The WARREN COURT *and the* CONSTITUTION

The
WARREN COURT
and the
CONSTITUTION

A Critical View of Judicial Activism

By JOHN DENTON CARTER

PELICAN PUBLISHING COMPANY
GRETNA 1973

Copyright © 1973
By John Denton Carter
All rights reserved

Book design by Oscar Richard
Jacket Design by Gerald Bower

Library of Congress Cataloging in Publication Data
Carter, John Denton.
　The Warren Court and the Constitution.

1. United States. Supreme Court. I. Title.
KF8748.C33　　　　　　　347'.73'26　　　　　　　73-7828
ISBN 0-911116-98-2

Manufactured in the United States of America by
Benson Printing Company, Nashville, Tennessee
Published by Pelican Publishing Company
630 Burmaster Street, Gretna, Louisiana 70053

To My Wife

Contents

Preface	ix
1 Earl Warren and the *Brown* Decision	3
2 Distorted Historical Record in the *Brown* Case	12
3 A Closeup View of the *Brown* Opinion	21
4 Tainted "Modern Authority" Cited in the *Brown* Case	30
5 The Law and the Prophets	40
6 Fourteenth Amendment: The First Phase	49
7 Fourteenth Amendment Transfigured	57
8 Fourteenth Amendment and the Bill of Rights	66
9 Internal Security and the Communists	75
10 Intellectuals and the Court	82
11 Underlying "Sham Spirituality"	90
12 Earl Warren, Heroic Lawgiver	101
13 Earl Warren, Constitutional Anarchist	112
14 Heritage of the New Deal	121
15 Abe Fortas Scandal	132
16 Educationists and the Schools	138
17 Loss of Faith in the Federal Courts	145
18 Can the Courts Be Contained?	155

Preface

HISTORY, THE SKEPTIC WARNS, is written by the survivors. Should the liberal faith survive these troubled times and continue to dominate the intellectual life of the nation, it can be assumed that the exalted place in American history already awarded our modern, politically activist Supreme Court will be secure. It is possible, however, that American historical scholarship will return to an older tradition of belief in rule by representative government rather than by a nonelected intellectual elite and its judicial collaborators. In such case, there will be little sympathy for the currently popular concept of judicial activism as a proper instrument for reforming the political and social order. In the future, no less than at present, the conservative view of the "Warren Revolution," as it has been called by L. Brent Bozell in his book of that title—or simply "Warrenism," as other critics have named this judicial venture into politics—will be less than flattering.

One certain verdict of conservative historians, if such survive, will be that Earl Warren and his colleagues could not have been the heroic reformers acclaimed by their liberal admirers, because the hero in history is always the leader rather than the follower or the prisoner of another's ambition. Members of the Warren Court had no independent will of their own but were prisoners of the will of the restless, ambitious, power-seeking leaders of the contemporary liberal-left coalition. This coalition was made up of the intellectual class—the verbalists of the academy, media, pulpit, and bureaucracies; their allies of the left-leaning special interest pressure groups such as the AFL-CIO, NAACP, ACLU, NEA, and NCC; subservient politicians; and utopian activists generally. It may be that history will judge that the Supreme Court under Earl Warren was little more than a transmission belt, a means of effecting a massive transfer of political power from elected representatives of the people at federal and especially state and local levels to this same liberal-left coalition.

A transmission of power must have taken place because after the *Brown* decision of 1954 the publishers of the Washington *Post* or the attorneys of the NAACP Legal Defense Fund or the members of the Harvard law faculty had more real authority over the school systems of the state of Alabama, say, or its police powers or its internal security arrangements than did the governor, the state legislature, the state courts, the school board members, or the hundreds of other elected state and local officials. Earl Warren and his colleagues, aided by earlier rulings of the New Deal Court, made this possible.

Our Supreme Court today has placed itself in a highly controversial and vulnerable political position, because it has given way to the pressures exerted upon it by liberal activists supported by the whole of the left political spectrum. In their drive for utopia, the liberal-left groups had been unable to work their will altogether with Congress and the executive and had therefore brought pressures to bear upon the Supreme Court, forcing it to subordinate its role as an impartial court of justice and to convert itself into a political power center in competition with the political branches and the elected state governments. Pressure from the left has driven the Court to the brink of constitutional anarchy, as evidenced by a 1968 speech of the then chief justice Earl Warren at New York University Law School in which he declared that the Supreme Court's essential function is "to act as a final arbiter of minority rights," and that the Court stood ready

Preface

to advance minority interests "if the executive and legislative branches falter."

It would be difficult to find a more confused statement of the duties of our highest court as laid down in the Constitution. Certain obvious questions come to mind immediately:

Where are the constitutional rights of the majority—the stable, productive, law-abiding, tax-paying members of the middle and working classes who provide the strength and continuity that sustain the national life?

What authority does the Court have to assume the duties of the other branches, and who is to determine if these branches have faltered? What has happened to the reserved rights of the states which lie at the heart of our constitutional system and without which the Constitution would never have been adopted?

How is the term "minority" to be defined? Does it include the farmers, the suburban middle class, the southern whites, or the Indians on reservations, each of which is a distinct economic or racial minority of the total population? Apparently not, because decisions of the Supreme Court in recent years seem to indicate that the term as used by Chief Justice Warren in his speech includes only the currently fashionable groups which the liberals have made the special objects of their affections. For the most part these groups possess a strong political leverage that can be controlled by the liberal leadership; but they include also unstable elements living on the fringes of society or outside the law who provide ideal objects for the outpourings of liberal pity.

The Warren Court, while posing as liberal, which in the older sense of the term meant belief in freedom, was actually reactionary in that its decisions tended to consolidate power in the central government, thereby restricting the freedom of the states, local governments, and the people. When the exercise of arbitrary power by a handful of appointed judges, acting as agents of private interest groups, is carried on in the name of freedom, then language has lost all meaning in this so-called democracy as it has in the Communist states.

Our politicized judiciary needs to be reminded of Thomas Hobbes' famous aphorism: "Freedom is political power divided into small fragments." It is not political power concentrated in the hands of a few appointed judges.

Our constitutional system has been subverted by the judicial tyranny that Jefferson feared, *i.e.*, the alleged superior wisdom of a small group of appointed judges over that of the thousands of elected representatives of the people in the federal, state, and local governments. Because the human thirst for power is insatiable, it is certain that this unlawful extension of the judicial authority will continue and become increasingly menacing to stable government and public order unless the Court is contained and forced to return to its prescribed duties under the Constitution.

The
WARREN COURT
and the
CONSTITUTION

1

Earl Warren and the *Brown* Decision

> Princes succeed one another; and one judge passeth, another cometh; nay, Heaven and Earth shall passe; but not one tit[t]le of the Law of Nature shall passe; for it is the Eternall Law of God. Therefore all the Sentences of precedent Judges that have ever been, cannot all together make a Law contrary to naturall Equity. . . .
>
> Thomas Hobbes, *Leviathan* (1651)

WHEN EARL WARREN took the oath of office as chief justice of the United States in October, 1953, there was little reason to believe that the Warren term, which was to last for sixteen years, would become one of the most politically turbulent and controversial periods in the history of the Supreme Court. Not since John Marshall's day, except in the uproar precipitated by the *Dred Scott* decision, and possibly in the short-lived New Deal assault on the judiciary, had the Court become the center of such bitter, harsh political recrimination. The quarrel over the political role assumed by the Warren Court shook the faith of many Americans in our constitutional system and in the continuing stability of the nation.

Rather than public expectation of a long period of political turmoil, the prevailing view in 1953 seemed to be that

Warren, a lifelong Republican and appointee of a Republican president, would place a halter on the politicized New Deal Court with its runaway tendencies. Warren began public life in his native California as a law-and-order man, a no-nonsense district attorney who became nationally famous as the prosecutor who sent to prison four maritime labor union agents charged with the murder of an anti-Communist member of the union. These men were not only condemned by Warren as murderers but also as "revolutionary radicals—Communists." It might be recalled that Warren's fellow Californian, Richard M. Nixon, also first gained national attention in an anti-Communist role, as an investigator of Communists in government while a member of the House of Representatives.

Warren's reputation as a vigorous prosecutor of Communist labor leaders who would employ any means, including murder, to eliminate active anti-Communist members of their union, led him to the attorney generalship of his state and to the governorship, to which he was elected three times, becoming one of the more popular holders of that office. His popularity as governor of California made him the Republican vice-presidential candidate on the Dewey ticket in 1948 and gave him an important role in the 1952 Republican convention that nominated Dwight D. Eisenhower and Richard M. Nixon. He supported Eisenhower in this convention and was awarded the chief justiceship.

There can be no doubt that Earl Warren's early political success was based on a solid conservative position, although he, like other Republican leaders in California, found it politically expedient to describe himself as a "progressive" Republican in the tradition of Theodore Roosevelt and Hiram Johnson. In 1941 Warren was publicly outraged by a decision of the California Parole Board, then controlled by liberal Democrats, to release three of the four labor union thugs whom he had sent to prison, but who had served only four years of twenty-year sentences. "The murderers are free today," Warren charged in a newspaper statement, "not because they are rehabilitated criminals but because they are politically powerful radicals."

This is the same Warren who later wrote the famous *Watkins* decision of the United States Supreme Court in which John T. Watkins, an Illinois labor leader, was freed by the Court after his conviction for contempt of Congress. In this case, Warren's role was reversed for it was he who was accused of favoring a convicted criminal because the latter was a politically powerful Communist radical. Watkins was certainly politically powerful because he had the vigorous support of the liberal press and the liberal left generally.

Why would Earl Warren, with his background, allow himself to become the ally and agent of the liberal-left groups that were determined to convert the Supreme Court into an instrument for bringing about revolutionary changes (Justice Abe Fortas described these changes as "revolutionary progress") in the political and social order? The answer might be found in a study of his career as attorney general and governor of California. After his initial success as a district attorney and prosecutor of Communist labor goons, Warren moved up the political ladder in state office in the guise of a nonpartisan above petty party struggles, stressing his "progressivism" rather than his Republicanism. As he strove to maintain a low profile as a Republican party man, he broadened his political base by gradually shifting his position to the left—by opening windows to the left, as this well-known tactic is sometimes described. By the time he ran for governor for a second term, he had shifted so far to the liberal side that he became the gubernatorial candidate not only of the Republican party but of the Democratic party as well. The latter had been controlled by the radical element of the state since 1934 when its nominee for governor had been the Socialist writer Upton Sinclair.

Earl Warren possessed considerable skill as a politician as proved by his ability to appeal to a very broad spectrum of the California electorate. While actually moving toward the Democratic left, he nevertheless retained his credentials and his public image as a Republican in good standing and in fact as an outstanding national leader of the party, as evidenced by his nomination for vice president in 1948 and his role in the victory of Eisenhower over Taft in the Republican convention of 1952. But when he moved to the Supreme Court in 1953 by appointment of Eisenhower, Warren threw aside his earlier middle-class Republicanism and his later nonpartisan stance. Much to the chagrin of Eisenhower and those conservatives who expected him to bring some balance to the New Deal Court, he took up a position alongside Hugo L. Black and William O. Douglas to form the extreme left wing of the Court.

Warren's opinions as chief justice and his speeches off the bench reflected a total rejection of his earlier conservatism and an unqualified acceptance of all of the utopian myths of modern liberalism—that all men are equal, that freedom and equality are compatible, that human nature is perfectible, that all human problems are susceptible to solution by governmental action, that virtue can be legislated or attained by court decree, and that the one redeeming human virtue is sympathy for the underdog, for the victims of society, real and imagined. All of these egalitarian ideas were implicit in Warren's court opinions and public statements. He had gone over completely to the liberal left and would remain a captive of the intellectuals and other liberal pressure groups for the whole of his career on the Court.

Although politically allied with the intellectual class while chief justice, and serving to a degree as one of its spokesmen on the Court, Warren was not an intellectual either in the true sense or in the present corrupt sense of the term. He was in fact a man of very commonplace mind whose attempts to formulate his ideas, especially in his public speeches while chief justice, sometimes approached the pathetic. All of the constitutional ideas that formed the intellectual underpinning of the Supreme Court under Warren's leadership were there when Warren arrived to take the oath of office as chief justice. They had come down by way of the New Deal Court and had been formulated to a large extent in the political and constitutional turbulence of the Reconstruction period and the post-World War I era which profoundly altered the power relationships of the federal and state governments.

This is not to say that Warren contributed nothing to the "Warren Revolution." Though he contributed no new ideas, he did supply the forceful leadership and sense of direction that led the Court away from its former hesitancy under the more moderate rule of Warren's predecessor, Chief Justice Fred M. Vinson of Kentucky, and turned the Court upon its headlong, devil-may-care activist course that marked the sixteen years of Warren's term.

During Warren's first year as chief justice, the Court handed down its unanimous decision in *Brown* v. *Board of Education* in which it declared unconstitutional all state laws requiring separation of the races in the public schools. Warren himself wrote the *Brown* opinion and no doubt exerted considerable influence in obtaining the approval of all members of the Court. This 1954 landmark decision was followed by many other controversial decrees, equally destructive of long-held constitutional principles, in the areas of internal security, criminal law, prayer and Bible reading in the schools, legislative apportionment, search and seizure, and the freedoms of press, speech, assembly and petition. But it was in the school segregation decree that the Warren Court took the plunge directly into the political and legislative thickets to bring about what it considered to be desirable social and political reforms and thereby introduced into the judicial process a sense of abandon that the New Deal Court had only approached.

L. Brent Bozell, in *The Warren Revolution* (Arlington House, 1966), and others have termed the Warren regime a revolution. Whether considered as a judicial, political, or social phenomenon, Warren's term was truly revolutionary and most notably in its effects upon the power relationships of the several branches of the federal government and the state governments as they were laid down in the Constitution. The decrees of the Warren Court, beginning with the *Brown* decision, resulted in a major seizure of power by the least representative branch of the federal government at the expense of the two elected branches—as well as the state and local governments, the state and local courts, the state and local law enforcement agencies, the school administrators, and the people themselves.

What the Court actually accomplished was a massive transfer of power from elected officials at federal, state, and local levels to those groups from whence the Court's political support came, that is, the groups which collectively have been described as the counter-government, made up of the intellectual class and allied special interest groups and, in general, utopian activists of the liberal left.

One of the more unfortunate legacies of the Warren regime was that it seriously diminished America's remaining faith in the Constitution as a shield against tyranny, in the great concept that the widest possible diffusion of power would be a sure protection of our liberties. Although the Constitution had been built around this concept, belief in its validity had eroded over the years as the powers of the central government grew at the expense of the states and the people. The Warren Court fairly well proved that it is an illusion after all, that it will not work when the central government, backed by superior force, fails to exercise self-discipline and self-restraint. Jefferson was surely right when he warned that a great weakness in our Constitution was the failure to provide proper safeguards against the enlargement of the powers of the federal government, including the judiciary, at the expense of the states and the people.

Yet all the blame for our present judicial predicament cannot be placed on the Supreme Court. The other two branches of the federal government, the executive and the legislative, aided the judicial power seizure either through direct action or through inaction. The two branches made no serious attempt to check the erosion of their own constitutional powers or to protect the states and the people from the unconstitutional encroachments of the Warren Court. They were more concerned with seeking the votes of the various groups that supported the Court's activism than in discharging their constitutional duties.

In a number of cases, it is true, conservatives in Congress attempted to put through remedial legislation to restrict the Court's appellate powers or proposed constitutional amendments to limit the Court's powers or to reverse its decisions, but in all cases the attempts were abortive. Congress has adequate constitutional means of limiting the Court's powers, but the congressional authority will not be exercised as long as Congress and the executive branch are moved, not by the interests of the majority of the people but by those of aggressive minority groups on the left. These groups hold the balance of power in many of the larger and some smaller states and thereby possess a political leverage, a swing vote, that gives them an advantage beyond that derived from mere numbers. Rather than limiting the Court's powers, Congress, at the urging of the executive, passed a series of laws vastly extending the power of the federal courts and the executive branch to coerce the states, local communities, and individuals in matters reserved to the states and the people by the Constitution.

One of the less glorious facts in recent United States history has been that the initial thrust of the Warren Court, the taking over of the schools, was accomplished at the point of the bayonet with the cooperation of a succession of presidents. Eisenhower set the precedent at Little Rock; he was followed by Kennedy at Oxford, Mississippi, and in Alabama. With these precedents, Johnson did not hesitate to force the use of troops to protect those bent on public disorder in the march from Selma to Montgomery, Alabama.

From all of the warped decisions of the Warren Court, serious consequences have followed. Some of the results have been: weakened internal security and police forces responsible for preserving internal order; a breakdown in law and order to such an extent that citizens are increasingly subject to criminal attack on person and property; federal court supervision of the public schools in the most minute details; massive dislocations of population; the flooding of the country with pornography; the downgrading of religious training of children in the public schools; and the intensification of the racial war, North as well as South.

Throughout much of the nation, especially in the large cities and the towns and rural regions of the South, the public school systems are staggering under the repeated blows of the federal courts, various departments of the executive branch, and a variety of private groups seeking utopian solutions for our racial problems, including some advocating violent solutions. In spite of these blows, most public schools will continue to operate for an indefinite period; but for many the vital spark that drives teachers to teach and pupils to learn has died, and education is no longer possible in the heat of racial and political turmoil, even with policemen patrolling the hallways.

A former superintendent of schools in Philadelphia, in testifying before a committee of Congress in 1971, warned that the "urban schools of this country are dying," principally because of "the lack of money and staff to provide even a basic education." And why are the urban schools short of money? It is largely because decrees of the federal courts since 1954 have degraded the tax base of the city schools by driving the affluent, tax-paying middle class out of the cities into the suburbs. The superintendent concluded that urban education is on the verge of collapsing, and once it does, he said, "the death of the great cities won't be very far behind."

And what will happen once our great cities die? Chaos will surely follow and Americans will then be wondering why our Supreme Court had given such overriding importance to what a leading liberal historian has described as "a loose phrase," by which he meant the "equal protection" clause of the Fourteenth Amendment, while virtually disregarding the purposes of the Constitution as stated in the preamble: "to form a more perfect union, establish justice, insure domestic tranquility, provide for the common defense, promote the general welfare, and secure the blessings of liberty to ourselves and our posterity." The Supreme Court under Earl Warren was not even concerned with establishing justice but was quite vigilant in granting special privileges to favored minorities and to those elements operating on the fringes of the law or without the law who demanded rights while rejecting all responsibilities.

2

Distorted Historical Record in the *Brown* Case

> If, in the opinion of the people, the distribution or modification of the constitutional powers be in any particular wrong, let it be corrected by an amendment in the way which the constitution designates. But let there be no change by usurpation, for though this, in one instance, may be the instrument of good, it is the customary weapon by which free governments are destroyed.
>
> George Washington, *Farewell Address* (1796)

BROWN V. BOARD OF EDUCATION OF TOPEKA, KANSAS, was one of a group of five school segregation cases brought up on appeal to the United States Supreme Court from the lower federal courts in the 1952–1953 session. They involved school segregation laws in four states and the District of Columbia. In these cases, the issue before the Court was whether separation of the races in the public schools by state or district law is in violation of the Constitution.

In the four cases involving state laws, NAACP counsel for the appellants argued that school segregation statutes are in violation of the "equal protection" clause of the Fourteenth Amendment. This argument had been rejected by the lower federal courts, citing earlier Supreme Court opinions upholding the "separate but equal" doctrine, and also citing the Tenth Amendment which reserves to the states or the people all powers not specifically delegated to the central government. Because the Fourteenth Amendment applies only to the states, the NAACP counsel based its arguments in the District of Columbia case, *Bolling* v. *Sharpe*, on the "due process" clause of the Fifth Amendment.

Brown and the related cases were first argued before the Supreme Court in December, 1952. At this time the Court was unable to make a decision and asked counsel on both sides for further argument. Because the Fourteenth Amendment makes no reference to schools, the Court requested counsel to direct its arguments to several constitutional questions, including the following: "What evidence is there that the Congress which submitted and the State legislatures and conventions which ratified the Fourteenth Amendment, contemplated or did not contemplate, understood or did not understand, that it would abolish segregation in the public schools?"

When the United States Supreme Court asked for further evidence as to the intentions of the framers of the Fourteenth Amendment with respect to school segregation, was it being honest and aboveboard? Did the Court truly want additional evidence to assist it in arriving at a correct constitutional decision, or had it already made up its mind? Was the Court searching for the truth or was it actually in collusion with the NAACP lawyers, asking them in effect to give the Court more ammunition so that it could make a *plausible* argument that segregation is unconstitutional under the Fourteenth Amendment? One of our leading liberal historians who has taken an active interest in "civil rights" had something revealing to say on these matters.

On December 28, 1961, Dr. Alfred H. Kelly, professor of history, Wayne State University, Detroit, Michigan, made a speech before a group of applauding historians at the annual meeting of the American Historical Association in Washington, D.C. With considerable relish, albeit with some inner squirming, Dr. Kelly told his audience of how he had debased his profession by lending his talents to the NAACP legal staff for the purpose of falsifying the historical record in the *Brown* case in order to give the United States Supreme Court the outward appearance of constitutional purity. He agreed to use his training as a historian, not to search for truth but to search for material that would assist the Supreme Court in hiding the truth.

When the Supreme Court asked counsel for further argument on the segregation cases, Thurgood Marshall, then head of the NAACP legal staff and later appointed to the Supreme Court by Lyndon B. Johnson, wrote Dr. Kelly, asking him to prepare a paper on the intent of the framers of the Fourteenth Amendment. Later, Dr. Kelly participated in a conference in New York called by the NAACP Legal Defense Fund, to which 125 liberal scholars—historians, constitutional lawyers, political scientists, and educators—had been invited. At this conference, it was generally agreed by the participants that the Supreme Court had already made up its mind, but that the Court wanted "a plausible historical argument" that the Fourteenth Amendment was intended by its authors to abolish school segregation.

The purpose of the conference of scholars was to draw up the historical portions of the brief that the NAACP counsel would present at the next session of the Court, the 1953-1954 session. Dr. Kelly explained the problem in these words:

> The problem we faced was not the historian's discovery of the truth, the whole truth and nothing but the truth; the problem instead was the *formulation of an adequate gloss* on the fateful events of 1866 [the year Congress passed the Civil Rights Act and approved the Fourteenth Amendment] sufficient to convince the Court that we had something of a historical case. . . .
>
> It is not that we were engaged in formulating lies; there was nothing so crude and naive as that. But we were *using facts, emphasizing facts, bearing down on facts, sliding off facts, quietly ignoring facts and above all in-*

terpreting facts in a way to do what Marshall said we had to do. . . . [emphasis added]

In discussing the nature of Dr. Kelly's research for the NAACP, it might be well to review briefly the background of the Fourteenth Amendment. It is significant that the Supreme Court's vast expansion of its powers in the *Brown* case was based largely on this tainted amendment to the Constitution which was forced upon the country by the Radical Republicans of the Reconstruction period. The political purpose of the Fourteenth Amendment and the Fifteenth Amendment that soon followed was to enfranchise the Negro and thereby strengthen Republican control over the central government and gain control of the state governments in the South. The Fourteenth Amendment made the Negro a citizen and gave him full legal rights; the Fifteenth Amendment gave him the vote. Thaddeus Stevens, the Radical Republican leader in the House, stated the purpose of his group bluntly: "to secure perpetual ascendancy to the party of the Union."

David Lawrence, to his great credit, long attempted in his newspaper column and in *U.S. News and World Report* to alert the people to the fact that the Fourteenth Amendment had been unconstitutionally adopted, has been a source of much judicial mischief, and should therefore be repealed. Mr. Lawrence referred to it as the "worst scandal in our history." The story of the Radical Republican tactics in securing the ratification of this amendment by the states has been told in nearly every school history of the United States, except, of course, those that have been produced in recent years in response to black power and liberal demands for the rewriting of American history.

In order to understand fully the thinking of Congress in approving the Fourteenth Amendment, it is necessary to examine the debates on the companion piece, the Civil Rights Act of 1866. Both the act and the supporting amendment were passed or approved by the 39th Congress in the 1865–1866 session. It was here, in the congressional record of the debates that Dr. Kelly began his research, for he knew, as he stated, that "the Fourteenth Amendment had evolved, in some considerable part, out of the Civil Rights Act of 1866." Dr. Kelly admitted that the debates in Congress contained more on school segregation than he had realized and that it "looked rather decidedly bad" from the NAACP point of view.

During the debates on the Civil Rights Act, some members of Congress expressed concern over the meaning of the rather ambiguous term "civil rights and immunities." Senator Trumbull of Illinois, who introduced the bill in the Senate, explained that civil rights meant no more than "the right to make and enforce contracts, to sue and be sued, and to give evidence, to inherit, purchase, sell, lease, hold and convey real and personal property." In other words, the act did not intend to assure absolute equality of conditions for whites and blacks, but only equality of legal rights; it proposed to establish the classic principle of justice, as defined by Hobbes, "giving to every man his own."

Some members of Congress were not satisfied with the attempts to clarify the term "civil rights and immunities" and expressed fears that the civil rights bill might outlaw segregated schools or interfere with state laws against racial intermarriage. They were given assurances on this by Representative Wilson of Iowa, chairman of the House Judiciary Committee. He explained that civil rights and immunities did not mean civil, social, and political equality of all citizens of whatever race or color, nor did it mean "their children shall attend the same schools." In the Civil Rights Act as passed, Congress avoided a radical interpretation of the term "civil rights and immunities" and gave it the limited meaning given it by Senator Trumbull. In the Fourteenth Amendment that followed, Congress used the term "privileges" rather than "civil rights." The pertinent section, cited by the Warren Court, read as follows: "No State shall make or enforce any law which shall abridge the privileges or immunities of citizens of the United States; nor shall any State deprive any person of life, liberty, or property, without due process of law, nor deny to any person within its jurisdiction the equal protection of the laws."

This is the broadly worded phrasing of the Fourteenth Amendment that the Warren Court gave as its authority for striking down the school segregation laws of the states. One other fact should be added to demonstrate that the Warren Court disregarded the intent of Congress. The same Congress that approved the Fourteenth Amendment passed a school measure which established segregated schools for Negroes in the District of Columbia.

In his address to the historians, Dr. Kelly stated: "The conclusion for any reasonably objective historian was painfully clear: The Civil Rights Act as it passed Congress was specifically rewritten to avoid the embarrassing question of a congressional attack upon state segregation laws, including school segregation." Nevertheless, Dr. Kelly and his fellow historians, lawyers, and political scientists, meeting in New York, did find a way of getting around the clear intent of the majority in Congress. They found that a minority of the Radical Republicans in Congress had favored a radical civil rights bill and a supporting constitutional amendment that would have abolished all forms of segregation of the races. Senator Jacob M. Howard of Michigan made the claim that the Fourteenth Amendment was intended to abolish "all class legislation in the States" and all "caste" injustices; but that was not the intent of the majority in Congress, and the amendment probably would not have been ratified by a single state outside of New England had it been given this meaning.

In preparing the historical portion of the NAACP brief, Dr. Kelly and his fellow historians and other scholars argued as follows:

> The Fourteenth Amendment, we told ourselves, had been necessary to accomplish a vast sweep of purpose far beyond the Civil Rights Act. Here we came down hard

on Howard's announcement that the purpose of the Amendment had been to abolish all class and caste in the United States. And we pounced on a phrase [of Congressman Bingham's in the debate on the Fourteenth Amendment] "that statutes are writ sharp and narrow and specific, but constitutions are writ broad for ages yet unborn."

In our mind's eye, Bingham almost seemed to be speaking for our purposes, saying to the Court in the twentieth century that if your age, far beyond our span of time, sees in this Amendment a new birth of liberty it will be altogether legitimate for you to use it for that purpose.

The Court did use this type of argument for overturning previous Court rulings which had held that segregation of the races was not forbidden by the Fourteenth Amendment. Thurgood Marshall told the historians and other scholars that he did not have to have an ironclad case but only enough ammunition to get a draw in the historical argument. He read the minds of the justices correctly, for in the *Brown* decision they claimed that the historical evidence was "inconclusive." If that were true, the logical move would have been to throw the suit out of court because the NAACP attorneys had not proved their case.

But the ways of the Warren Court are inscrutable. Having discarded the historical argument as inconclusive, although retaining the Fourteenth Amendment as its basic authority, the Court shifted over to sociological grounds. It decided the case on questionable data of certain leftist social scientists and on the basis of personal sentiments of the justices. The Court had lost all sense of reality and handed down its decision out of a dream world of wishful thinking that human nature could be changed by judge-made law. The members of the Court had ceased to be judges and become social engineers, assuming the role of what philosopher George Santayana, onetime Harvard professor, described as "heroic reformers." While claiming to bring justice, they brought, in time, disintegration and chaos. A "new birth of liberty" indeed! Leviathan never confers liberty on a people, as many Americans have learned.

And what of Dr. Kelly? Has he enjoyed any academic freedom of late? Has he had any black militants visiting his classrooms checking up on the purity of his ideology and his adherence to black power demands in his history lectures? Is he secure in his person and property, or have his home and family been threatened? From numerous news reports, the evidence is conclusive that many of Dr. Kelly's fellow liberals in the northern and western universities, and some southern, have had trouble. Disruptions of classrooms and threats of physical attack by the black militants and their New Left allies may have convinced some of the liberal professors that violence to the Constitution can have some strange side effects.

Whatever his thoughts are today, Dr. Kelly's conscience was twitching badly as he prepared his first paper for the NAACP legal staff back in 1953. In his own words, he was trying to be both historian and advocate and found that the combination was not a very good one. He bared his soul to his fellow historians at the 1961 meeting in Washington: "I was facing, for the first time in my own career, the deadly opposition between my professional integrity as a historian and my wishes and hopes with respect to a contemporary question of values, of ideals, of policy, of partisanship and of political objectives. I suppose if a man is without scruple, this matter will not bother him, but I am frank to say that it bothered me terribly."

Dr. Kelly gave up his appointed role in society, just as the members of the Supreme Court had done, to become a "heroic reformer" who would radically change or destroy the established order to build a new order based on his personal ideas of justice and morality. But his liberal dream world is rapidly becoming, as Santayana predicted, one of "moral disintegration," "intellectual chaos," and "internecine war." That is a fair description of the trends in our society today, and considerable blame belongs to our Supreme Court and those liberal intellectuals and their allies who drove the Court on to its destructive course of trying to cure our social and political ills by judicial fiat instead of performing its prescribed duties under the Constitution.

A Closeup View
of the *Brown* Opinion

> We are afraid to put men [including judges] to live and trade each on his own private stock of reason; because we suspect that the stock in each man is small, and that individuals would do better to avail themselves of the general bank and capital of nations and of ages.
>
> Edmund Burke, Reflections on the
Revolution in France (1790)

MEMBERS OF THE WARREN COURT and its defenders off the bench often charged that the Court's critics did not read the full text of the arguments supporting its decisions but relied on fragmentary newspaper reports briefly summarizing the decisions. The usual conclusion was that if the critic would take the time to read the full text of the opinion in any of the numerous controversial cases, then he would understand and approve of what the Court had really said and would not be "shooting from the hip," to quote the Washington *Post*, which had appointed itself special guardian of Earl Warren and the Warren Court.

Agnes Meyer of the family that owns the *Post*, commenting on the controversial *Schempp-Murray* cases in a speech in 1965, stated that "if more thinking people merely read" the Court's opinion in these cases, "the careless abuse heaped upon our highest Court would disappear." But did Agnes Meyer read the text of the Court's argument or its historical inquiry into the background of these cases? Apparently not, for there was no argument or inquiry. The justices merely handed down two declarations to the effect that the Court had already settled in earlier opinions the juridical principles involved and cited the precedent cases. The Court concluded that any further questioning of the "history, logic and efficacy" of its position would be "of value only as academic exercises." The Agnes Meyer speech and the Court's decision together present a very good example of the hypocrisy of the Court's liberal defenders and the arrogance and insensitivity of the Court in matters deeply affecting the American people, for these cases involved prayer and Bible reading in the public schools.

If Agnes Meyer and her "thinking people," meaning the liberal defenders of the Court, had taken the trouble to read the Court's opinion in the case of *Brown* v. *Board of Education,* they would never again have asked the public to read the full text of a Warren Court decree, especially if it were an opinion written by Warren himself. The *Brown* opinion is so lacking in moral and intellectual respectability that it may go down in judicial history as the shoddiest performance of the United States Supreme Court in 165 years. It is shoddy, whether viewed as rhetoric, ethics, history, logic, or constitutional law.

In the preceding chapter an account has been given of the collusion between the Supreme Court, the NAACP legal staff, and a group of liberal historians and other scholars in distorting the historical record so that the Court could throw it aside and claim, with a straight face, that the record was "inconclusive." Having done this in the earlier part of the *Brown* opinion, the Court then presented a comparison of public schools of 1868 and those of the present; this comparison was wholly irrelevant to the case at hand and was,

A Closeup View of the Brown Opinion

in fact, no more than window dressing, as Bozell has pointed out in *The Warren Revolution*. In making the transition from the subject of the intentions of the framers of the Fourteenth Amendment to a comparison of the status of public education in 1868 and today, the Warren Court perpetrated some of the muddiest rhetoric and falsest logic to be found in the annals of the Court. The transition paragraph opened with a *non sequitur* in this muddy sentence: "An additional reason for the inconclusive nature of the [Fourteenth] Amendment's history, with respect to segregated schools, is the status of public education at that time."

The paragraph ended on a wholly false statement as shown in Chapter 2 of this work. The statement is as follows: "As a consequence, it is not surprising that there should be so little in the history of the Fourteenth Amendment relating to its intended effect on public education."

The fact is, there is much more on this subject in the record of the debates in the 39th Congress and subsequent interpretations by the Supreme Court than the Warren Court was willing to admit. As described in Chapter 2, Dr. Alfred H. Kelly, a historian employed by the NAACP to write a paper on the intent of the framers of the Fourteenth Amendment, found much more on the subject of school segregation than he had anticipated. During the debates on the Civil Rights Act, out of which the Fourteenth Amendment had evolved, the Republican leaders in Senate and House were forced to assure the Congress that the act did not intend to assure absolute equality of conditions for whites and blacks but only legal equality; it did not mean that "their children shall attend the same schools." This same Congress soon afterward established a segregated school for Negroes in the District of Columbia.

After completing the public schools historical survey, the Court moved over into sociological theories:

> In approaching this problem, we cannot turn the clock back to 1868 when the [Fourteenth] Amendment was

adopted, or even to 1896 when Plessy v. Ferguson was written. We must consider public education in the light of its full development and its present place in American life throughout the nation. *Only in this way* can it be determined if segregation in the public schools deprives the plaintiffs of the equal protection of the laws. [emphasis added]

"Only in this way" indeed! The Court is saying that the cases can be decided only upon the Court's own views as to the importance of public education in American life and not upon the Constitution and legal precedent.

The whole statement is filled with spurious reasoning. In the first place, why shouldn't the Court turn the clock back to the appropriate debates in Congress and to subsequent Court decisions as it had been doing for a century and a half? This is the most elemental duty of appellate judges, as James J. Kilpatrick has pointed out. In the *Brown* case it should have examined carefully and honestly the intent of the framers of the Fourteenth Amendment and consulted the Court's decisions on this same subject since 1868. In these decisions the Court had said that the Fourteenth Amendment did not intend to prohibit segregated schools. Other decisions said that the Tenth Amendment made education the business of the states. Furthermore, there was no need to go back all the way to 1868 and 1896. Had the Court turned the clock back only four years, it would have found itself holding that segregated schools were not in violation of the Constitution.

In the second place, the Court was perfectly willing to turn the clock back when that suited its own purposes. In the Little Rock case of *Cooper* v. *Aaron,* for example, in which the Warren Court made its most extreme claims to power, the Court turned the clock back all the way to 1803 when John Marshall was chief justice and cited *Marbury* v. *Madison* which, the Court said, "declared the basic principle that the Federal judiciary is supreme in the exposition of the law of the Constitution." *Marbury* v. *Madison* was an extremely controversial decision in its time, was roundly condemned by President Thomas Jefferson, and has been questioned by other presidents, members of Congress, and constitutional scholars. The Court might have added that John Marshall also said in a later decision that the Supreme Court did not have the power to make the law, only to interpret it. Here are Marshall's words: "Courts are the mere instruments of the law, and can will nothing. . . . Judicial power is never exercised for the purpose of giving effect to the will of the judge, always for the purpose of giving effect to the will of the Legislature; or, in other words, to the will of the law."

The real purpose of the "we cannot turn the clock back" paragraph was boldly to cast aside law and precedent and to lay the groundwork for making an unconstitutional decision based on the views and sentiments of the justices with the support of questionable authorities in the social sciences. The justices dropped all pretense of standing above the political struggles of the day and became at once politicians, social engineers, and lawgivers.

As sugarcoating, the justices followed up their decision not to set the clock back with a few sanctimonious educationist cliches, right out of the works of the Socialist John Dewey, or one of his Columbia colleagues, about the importance of public education such as: it is "indispensable" to "our democratic society"; it is "the very foundation of good citizenship"; it is "a principal instrument in awakening the child to cultural values" and "in helping him to adjust normally to his environment." These are largely non-thoughts of questionable validity. The public schools, we now know, are too often the incubators of moral and intellectual monsters.

Even less valid was the Court's statement that "education is perhaps the most important function of state and local governments." Education may be the most expensive, but the principal functions of state and local governments are to preserve law and order and to protect the lives and property of the citizens. Without these, an orderly, civilized society cannot exist. Education is an incidental and very recent function of government; it is the belief of many that education is better carried on in religious and other private schools. Ironically, the Warren Court has been a major factor in advancing the view of the superiority of private schools among many groups and individuals who had previously held the liberal view that the public schools are God's principal agency on earth.

With the sugarcoating out of the way, the Court was now ready to make its decision on "intangible considerations," supported by "modern authority." The key sentences in the opinion were as follows:

> To separate [Negro children] from others of similar age and qualifications solely because of their race generates a feeling of inferiority as to their status in the community that may affect their hearts and minds in a way unlikely ever to be undone. . . .
> We conclude that in the field of public education the doctrine of "separate but equal" has no place. Separate educational facilities are inherently unequal.

The Court concluded that the Negro plaintiffs had been "deprived of the equal protection of the laws guaranteed by the Fourteenth Amendment." The justices had reversed every Supreme Court decision on this subject since 1868—and there were many, including one as late as 1950—and had substituted its own sentiments based on one factor alone, the purported effect of segregated schools on the feelings of Negro children. Did the Court give any thought to the probable effect of the decree on the feelings of white children forced to attend integrated schools as guinea pigs in a sociological experiment? Or the effect on white and black parents who feared for the health and safety of their children in the hostile racial atmosphere which they knew would develop and which has developed? Did the Court consider that the NAACP legal staff may have been speaking for only a small group of Negro political activists and intellectuals and not the great majority of the Negro people who preferred their own neighborhood schools and teachers of their own race just as the whites did? The *Brown* opinion was not based on a sound knowledge of Negro aspirations and Negro-white relationships but on the corrupted data of a small group of New York-based, left-wing social scientists.

The Warren Court, in its cocksureness, was certain that only good would flow from its altruism, without considering that the decision might bring inflamed racial tensions, public disorder, and anarchy in the schools. The Court failed to anticipate the massive shifts in population as the whites—including many liberal lawmakers and some judges in Washington—attempted to escape from the effects of the *Brown* and later decisions on race mixing in the schools. Much evil has issued from the benevolent thoughts and acts of ideologues who would remake society in accordance with their own small private stock of wisdom and moral sense. The members of the Warren Court were acting not as judges but as advocates, as were all of the authorities they cited who, while posing as objective scholars, were trying to bring about utopia—or, in the words of one of the authorities cited, upholding "an audacious conception of education which glows with the magnetic vision of an order in which all people are at last equal and free, not merely in theory, but in every aspect of day by day practice." Freedom cannot exist in an authoritarian society in which the government attempts to enforce equality by law or court decree.

The collective "modern authority" whose works were cited in the *Brown* opinion and listed in its footnote 11 contained a mare's nest of social scientists who were specialists in those flimsiest of disciplines—sociology, psychology, and cultural anthropology. They were primarily political partisans of what they believed to be the Negro cause. While some of them were Negroes, many of them were white liberals, a term employed contemptuously by black militants today.

Before discussing in the next chapter the identity, background, and work of the so-called "modern authority" cited in *Brown,* it might be well first to bring out two important points about the Court's use of these authorities:

(1) The works of these authorities listed in footnote 11 of the *Brown* decision were not introduced as evidence in the litigation before the Supreme Court. After listening to or reading millions of words of argument in the areas of constitutional law, the history of the adoption of the Fourteenth Amendment, and the intentions of the framers of both the Fourteenth and the Fifth Amendments, the Court threw all of these out the window and pulled from under the table the treatises of the social scientists cited as authorities and based the *Brown* opinion on these. The attorneys representing the states, including John W. Davis, one of the ablest constitutional lawyers then living, were suddenly faced with a *fait accompli* and were given no opportunity to refute the arguments or findings in the treatises of the social scientists. Professor Peter A. Carmichael of Louisiana State University stated that the failure to give the defense attorneys the opportunity to cross-examine the so-called authorities cited by the Court was "in violation of the most elementary idea of justice. . . ."

(2) Only two years before the *Brown* decision, in April, 1952, the Supreme Court had handed down a decision written by Justice Frankfurter and concurred in by Chief Justice Vinson and Associate Justices Burton, Clark, and Minton. In this decision the Court rejected the social sciences as competent authorities in the areas of race relations and constitutional law. Here is what Justice Frankfurter wrote:

> Only those lacking responsible humility will have a confident solution for problems as intractable as the frictions attributable to differences of race, color, or religion. . . . Certainly the due-process clause does not require the legislature to be in the vanguard of science—especially sciences as young as human psychology and cultural anthropology. . . .

It is not within our competence to confirm or deny claims of social scientists as to the dependence of the individual on the position of his racial or religious group in the community.

In this opinion, the Supreme Court was unable to relate the findings of the social scientists to the claims of racial and religious minority groups under the Constitution; but two years later the Court set forth as authorities in the *Brown* opinion the subjective views of a group of leftist social scientists, citing as a constitutional basis for the opinion the Fourteenth Amendment in the state cases and the Fifth Amendment in the District of Columbia case.

What had happened within these two years to cause the Court to reverse itself? There is little doubt that the death of Chief Justice Vinson and the appointment of Earl Warren as his successor had had some effect on the Court's aboutface. But what had happened to Frankfurter, Burton, Minton, and Clark? Were they too weak to resist the pressures and demands of political and racial groups and the pressures from the new chief justice and the more radical members of the Court? That could well have been the case, although we cannot be sure until the full record is revealed at some time in the future.

4

Tainted "Modern Authority" Cited in the *Brown* Case

> What we are now witnessing, in truth, is the final bankruptcy of the social sciences, as they are currently studied and taught in American universities. To see what is meant here, it is only necessary to think back to 1954, to the cruelly false hopes that were raised by the Supreme Court's decision desegregating the schools.
> ... there was bad science behind the raising of those false hopes. Desegregation and school integration were in fact offered as cure-alls, when they were nothing of the sort.
> Joseph Alsop, leading liberal journalist, in his column of May 28, 1969

AT SOME FUTURE TIME in our history—when legal scholarship in our leading law schools is no longer dominated by liberal ideologues, when judges have been made to return to their prescribed duties under the Constitution, and when "civil rights" agitators "of litigious dispositions and unquiet minds" (to borrow a phrase from Edmund Burke) are no longer allowed to clutter the court dockets with their trumped-up cases—legal historians from bench, bar and academy will look back in wonder that the Supreme Court of the United States would base a far-reaching decision affecting the welfare of millions of school children on such tainted "authority" as that cited in the *Brown* decree. This assumes, of course, that our constitutional system will survive and recover its old authority, our courts will continue to adjudicate, and our law schools will remain open in the face of the fierce attacks of the destructive forces that the Warren Court has helped to let loose over our land.

It is not surprising that the justices of the Warren Court would accept the corrupted data of the psychologists, sociologists, and cultural anthropologists when it is realized that the eastern law schools, which have exercised such a malign influence on the Supreme Court, are permeated with the same dogmatic liberalism of the social sciences, described in the law schools as "legal realism." These law schools, dominated by legal activists, have been the principal source of corruption in American jurisprudence from the 1920s through the New Deal era and on into the present period. Justice Frankfurter had been for many years a professor at the Harvard law school, and Justice Douglas had been on the faculty of the Yale law school. Other justices had served as summer lecturers in the law schools. Most of the law clerks serving the Supreme Court justices had for long come out of the Ivy League schools and a few Midwest and Far West law schools. Many of them returned to the law schools as teachers, thus carrying on an inbreeding process that assured the dominance of the judicial activist philosophy in the schools and in the courts.

The "modern authority" cited by the Supreme Court to buttress its decision in the *Brown* case consisted of two distinct groups of social scientists. In the first group were the authors of six short treatises listed in footnote 11 of the *Brown* opinion, most of these being articles from professional journals, although one was an unpublished manuscript. Following the listing of these works in footnote 11, the Court added: "And see generally Myrdal, *An American Dilemma* (1944)." The Myrdal study was a composite work which contained contributions from a number of social scientists hired as assistants to Myrdal by the Carnegie Foundation, the sponsor of the study.

The strong criticism that has been directed at the authorities cited in *Brown* has brought into question both their political loyalty and their professional competence. Most of these social scientists were Marxist in their political views, and many had been at one time or another members of the Communist party or of pro-Communist groups declared to be subversive by the attorney general of the United States. As to their professional competence, critics have maintained that their work was not scientific or objective but a mishmash of political ideology, pseudo-scientific opinion, manipulated data, and false reasoning.

The political background of the Court's authorities was exposed, for the first time in detail, by Senator James O. Eastland of Mississippi in a Senate speech of May 26, 1955. Senator Eastland, for many years chairman of the Senate Judiciary Committee, had been deeply concerned with the Supreme Court's increasingly activist political role and its encroachment upon the legislative power and the reserved powers of the states. In looking into the backgrounds of the so-called authorities, Senator Eastland was shocked by their Marxist leanings and their active roles in a variety of leftist organizations. Theodore Brameld, author of one of the treatises listed by the Court, was found to have been a member of ten organizations declared to be communistic, Communist-front, or Communist-dominated. His name had frequently appeared in a favorable light in the news columns of the *Daily Worker,* then the organ of the Communist party of the United States. In the case of Dr. E. Franklin Frazier, a professor of sociology at Howard University in Washington, D.C., the files of the House Un-American Activities Committee contained eighteen citations of his connection with Communist causes.

Senator Eastland's research revealed that Dr. Kenneth B. Clark, author of one of the studies cited by the Court, was an employee of the NAACP, the organization that supplied the legal staff to represent the plaintiffs in the school segregation cases. "To say the least," Senator Eastland remarked, "it is the most unusual procedure for any court to accept a litigant's paid employee as an authority on anything. . . ."

In looking at the backgrounds of Gunnar Myrdal and his assistants, Senator Eastland found an even more dismal picture. Mr. Myrdal himself was a Swedish Socialist politician and social scientist on the faculty of a Swedish university; he had had no experience with and little knowledge of the race problem in the United States. The Carnegie Foundation claimed that he was selected for that reason and that he would bring a fresh viewpoint to bear on the problem. It is more likely that the real reason Myrdal was selected was that the social engineers who controlled the Carnegie Foundation wanted a fellow traveller of the left who would bring forth a product that would reflect their own views and would exert a pro-Negro influence on American opinion.

Gunnar Myrdal, the Swedish Marxist ideologue, was wholly contemptuous of the American constitutional system, as he frankly indicated in *An American Dilemma.* He stated in this work that the Constitution of the United States was "unpractical and unsuited to modern conditions" and that its adoption was "nearly a plot against the common people." It is worth speculating as to the extent to which this two-volume study of the American Negro was actually consulted by the justices on the Court at the time of the *Brown* decree. Probably the more doctrinaire liberals such as Douglas, Frankfurter, and Black had some firsthand knowledge of the work since the true liberal must keep up to date on his ideology, and they were doubtless familiar with the political backgrounds of Myrdal and his fellow contributors. As for Warren, however, who was not a scholar, it is doubtful that he really understood what was in the work and who wrote it. It is conceivable that Warren's law clerks furnished him with a list of "authorities," including the Myrdal study, to attach to the decision to give it an aura of scholarship. Perhaps some day, when legal scholarship has been rescued from its prison, objective scholars will attempt to discover how our highest Court could so expose its intellectual laziness and careless use of questionable source materials.

When Senator Eastland saw the names of the "social experts" hired as assistants to Myrdal, he reached the conclusion that they had been deliberately selected from membership lists of communistic and Communist-front organizations. Probably the most conspicuous name on the list of contributors to Gunnar Myrdal's work was W.E.B. Du Bois, Negro sociologist, journalist, and political agitator who had written many portions of the study. Du Bois had been a member of a dozen or more subversive organizations during his long career with the NAACP. In the post-World War II period he formally joined the Communist party and moved to the African Republic of Ghana (then ruled by the despotic Nkrumah) where he died in 1963 at an advanced age. His memory has been honored by student Communists in American colleges and universities who named their campus organizations W.E.B. Du Bois clubs. Other Negro Communists or members of Communist-front groups who aided Myrdal were Doxie Wilkerson, Charles S. Johnson, James E. Jackson, Jr., and here again, Dr. E. Franklin Frazier. Not one single Negro conservative or moderate was called upon for assistance; they were all selected from the far left.

Almost as conspicuous as Du Bois, and probably more influential, was Frank Boas, founder of the Columbia University school of cultural anthropology and no doubt the one man who had done more than any other to corrupt the social sciences in American universities. Professor Boas was an immigrant from Germany where his parents had been active Marxist Socialists. In his academic career in the United States he took up the cause of the American Negro and spent a lifetime of agitation for "civil rights" and against "racism," meaning, of course, the other man's racism, not his own. He was appointed professor of anthropology at Columbia University in 1899 and became the leading proponent of cultural or environmental anthropology in the United States until he retired in 1936. Boas and his disciples, who today dominate the anthropology departments in American universities, have saturated the American mind with their environmental dogma and stand ready to tear to pieces any scholar who suggests that there are inherited physical and mental differences among the races.

One of the targets of their fierce attacks has been Dr. Arthur R. Jensen of the University of California who published a 1969 article in the *Harvard Educational Review* presenting evidence of differential intelligence among races. Dr. Jensen wrote that individual differences in intelligence are "predominantly attributable to genetic differences, with environmental factors contributing a minor portion." This was a denial of all that the Boas school had been teaching for two-thirds of a century. It is not surprising that the members of the American Anthropological Association were quite perturbed when they met in their annual convention in New Orleans in November, 1969. Professor Jensen's thesis was considered in papers read by five scholars at the session. Not one member of the panel of five defended the Jensen thesis or his right to hold it, and only two members of the large audience—and these two were psychologists rather than anthropologists—expressed sympathy for the Jensen view. Several speakers dismissed Jensen's thesis as "racism," and one referred to him as a "chauvinist, biased racist." Dr. Jensen had accused the anthropologists of "an emotionally based humanitarianism," and they proved at the New Orleans convention that the criticism was justified.

Frank Boas was a man of the far left and during his lifetime belonged to a long list of organizations found to be subversive. They are listed in Senator Eastland's speech and were taken from the files of the House Un-American Activities Committee, renamed in 1969 the House Internal Security Committee.

Chief Justice Warren's "modern authority" cited in the *Brown* opinion has been analyzed in some detail by Professor Peter A. Carmichael of Louisiana State University in his book *The South and Segregation* (Washington, D.C.; Public Affairs Press, 1965). Although Professor Carmichael found that the social science studies cited by Warren were not wholly without merit, they were generally filled with subjective opinion, manipulated data, false assumptions, and bad logic.

First on Warren's list of authorities was an unpublished study by Dr. Kenneth B. Clark, a Negro psychologist of the College of the City of New York, and, as mentioned earlier, an employee of the NAACP. This study had come out of the 1950 Midcentury White House Conference on Children and Youth—a typical promotion scheme of the liberal politicians, bureaucrats, minority groups, and intellectuals to stage a major propaganda venture at public expense. There was nothing in the Clark study to prove or disprove the *Brown* thesis that school segregation has a damaging psychological effect on Negro children. Dr. Clark was concerned with children of pre-school age. He attempted to prove that children very early become aware of racial differences, as early as the age of three. Dr. Clark carried out an experiment using dolls of varying shades of darkness to test the children's preferences. Since both white and black children seemed to prefer the lighter dolls, Dr. Clark concluded that the children had already developed "negative attitudes" toward the Negro and that "Negro subjects, when required to make racial identifications, generally reacted with behavior indicative of uneasiness, tension, or evasion, while there was no similar tendency among the whites."

The second "authority" on the Warren list also originated in the 1950 White House Conference. It is Chapter VI, "The Effects of Prejudice and Discrimination," from a book, *Personality in the Making,* which digested the contributions of more than a hundred participants in the conference. The editors of this volume, Helen L. Witmer and Ruth Kotinsky, also wrote Chapter VI cited in the *Brown* opinion. In the preface of the volume and in Chapter VI there is an admirable humility which acknowledges the inadequacy of the data and the methodology. The authors quote from Otto Klineberg's *Characteristics of the American Negro:* "Completely satisfactory research in this field will have to wait until psychologists have devised more adequate measures for the study of personality." And in Chapter VI of their study they acknowledge: "All who work in the fields pertaining to child life and child development are acutely aware of great chasms of ignorance."

The very tentative nature of the data presented in Chapter VI and the volume as a whole is indicated by the frequent use of qualifying terms such as "may be," "is likely," "seems," and "appears." Professor Carmichael warns in his book: "A careful reader will discount the whole accordingly. Nevertheless, the Supreme Court offers it as authoritative evidence for its proposition that segregated schools are detrimental to negro pupils."

The fact is, the data presented in the Court-cited Chapter VI are so tentative and inconclusive that one is led to suspect that the Court used Chapter VI, as well as some of the other sources cited in footnote 11, only as window dressing. If the Court's "authorities" proved anything, it was that the source of Negro feelings of inferiority was not the public school system alone or primarily, but American society as a whole. The Court might well have used this conclusion to find that separate schools for Negroes might be of benefit to them by making it possible for them to avoid integrated schools where contact with the whites caused damage to the Negro personality. This appears to be in accord with the thinking of many black militant groups today.

A review of the other "authorities" cited by Chief Justice Warren would be largely repetitious except in one case which has a unique feature. This study, published in the *Journal of Psychology* in 1948, six years before the *Brown* decision, was designed specifically to influence the Supreme Court and to persuade it to make up its mind that segregated schools and other public facilities were unconstitutional. Its purpose, not at all scholarly but wholly political, was "to gather material which would be relevant to a court decision" on "the legality of enforced segregation, regardless of equal facilities," a decision which "has not yet been rendered by the Supreme Court."

The study was promoted by a commission of the American Jewish Congress and was prepared by Max Deutscher and Isidor Chein under the title "The Psychological Effects of Enforced Segregation: A Survey of Social Science Opinion." It was based on a poll of 849 social scientists (sociologists, psychologists, and anthropologists), nearly all of them American. A questionnaire was sent out to each of these social scientists with a letter which stated the purpose to be that of "providing legislative bodies, courts and the general public with a consensus of responsible scientific opinion." The social scientists were asked to signify their approval of one of three statements which boil down to: (1) I believe enforced segregation to be bad; (2) I believe enforced segregation to be good; (3) I have no opinion. Note there is no room for the point of view held by many Americans, white and black, that the question is not whether separate schools are good or bad, but whether at this point in time they are necessary to preserve racial peace, a sense of racial community, and public order.

To ask these questions of the social scientists on the faculties of our colleges and universities is much like polling the black clergy as to whether Dr. Martin Luther King was a good man or a bad man. It is not at all surprising that over 90 percent of those who answered the questionnaire expressed the belief that enforced segregation was bad. Only 3 percent would admit that their opinions were based on personal views, value judgments, ethics, or moral belief. Most claimed that their opinions were grounded in research, either theirs or that of others.

To claim that the views of American social scientists on separation of the races in the schools represented "responsible scientific opinion" was wholly irresponsible and unscientific. Such opinion is no more scientific than the work of the social scientists themselves. The great majority of American social scientists on our campuses are highly prejudiced against conservative points of view, including opposition to enforced racial congregation by the federal government. However, many may have recently changed their minds as they go about their campuses in fear of life and limb, and as the black militants and members of the New Left disrupt their classes and threaten to burn down their storied halls.

The flimsy disciplines of social science could be useful tools of inquiry if employed by scholars of a philosophic or scientific turn of mind; but under the dominance of our leftist intellectuals they have become vastly corrupted. A close look at the Boas school of anthropology, mentioned earlier in this chapter, is enough to arouse skepticism in any honest mind. For decades the members of this school have not attempted to search for the truth about the races of mankind, but have been strenuously engaged in trying to prove as truth a false assumption that preceded research in the field.

5

The Law and the Prophets

> The question . . . is: shall the clear and ordinary meaning of words be followed or disregarded? The written Constitution stands like a tablet on Mt. Sinai, reading, "This is the law." The problem is to keep the law in the custody of prophets who know how to read the language of liberty.
>
> Irving Brant, *The Bill of Rights, Its Origin and Meaning* (Bobbs-Merrill, 1965)

> Here [in the Supreme Court decision in the Pentagon Papers case] is a supreme example of the problems we pose for ourselves by turning every political question—and some ethical questions—into judicial questions. . . . All of these questions are too complicated for judicial solution under the formal procedures of courts and the guidance of sibylline phrases such as "contracts and combinations in restraint of trade," "liberty of contract," "equal protection of the laws," "interstate commerce," and so on. . . .
>
> Dean Acheson, "The Purloined Papers," New York *Times*, July 7, 1971

HERE ARE TWO CLEARLY IRRECONCILABLE VIEWS of the Constitution and the problem of its interpretation. Irving Brant, in his work on the Bill of Rights, sees no great problem in interpretation. It is simply a matter of whether "the clear and ordinary meaning of words be followed or disregarded."

Mr. Brant has been one of the more ardent upholders of the Warren Court (the "most enlightened" in American history as it moved against "the blind forces of prejudice and apathy"). He is here attempting to establish himself and his fellow liberals as strict constructionists, just as the liberal press has attempted to portray the late Justice Hugo L. Black as the "Great Strict Constructionist" on the Court, going about the marble halls with his "thumb-worn" copy of the Constitution and shouting to all and sundry that "no law means no law" in the First Amendment—but not bothering to comment on whether "Congress means Congress" in the same amendment.

Of course, not all are able to grasp the clear meaning of the sacred inscription. Elsewhere in the book cited, Mr. Brant asserts that the part of the Constitution known as the Bill of Rights has been "the victim of prejudice and passion, among the active minority, abetted by ignorance and passivity among the majority" of Americans. But to the "prophets who know how to read the language of liberty" the meaning is clear enough; and these prophets (or "priest-interpreters" of the "sacred court," as Professor Jeffrey Hart of Dartmouth, a leading conservative, has called them) are capable of supplying ready and infallible answers. These prophets or priest-interpreters are none other than those members of the Supreme Court who have accepted the guidance of the liberal-left intellectuals as to the true meaning of the Constitution, especially the meaning of the "due process" and "equal protection" clauses of the Fourteenth Amendment. These two clauses form the basis for the prevailing revolutionary concept of constitutional construction which has led to such aberrations as the death of God in the public schools, the busing madness, and the bizarre claim of former Chief Justice Earl Warren that the essential function of the Supreme Court is "to act as a final arbiter of minority rights," thus implying a denial of constitutional rights and of justice to the majority when these are in conflict with minority claims to special privileges.

Irving Brant's views undoubtedly reflect those of a substantial element of the intellectual class and of liberals generally, although there have been dissenters, especially in the academy, who insist upon a more intellectually respectable defense of Supreme Court activism. Supporting the Brant view, one of the liberal news weeklies expressed the opinion that the Supreme Court "approaches the level of a sacred institution with its own broad but unique standards. . . ." There can be no doubt that those self-appointed keepers of the liberal conscience, the New York *Times* and Washington *Post,* would agree with this sacred image of the Court.

One of the more brazen attempts to clothe judicial activism with the sanctions of religion came from the pen of one-time Justice Abe Fortas in an article in the New York *Times* of November 28, 1972. It is ironic that this would come from Fortas, probably the most controversial figure ever to sit on the Supreme Court, who was forced to resign by public pressure for his questionable financial dealings. In an attempt to justify the Warren Court's "rediscovery of the human values which our Constitution states," Fortas oracularly proclaimed that our constitutional system's

> mandates are couched in terms of stern and absolute principle, structured upon the unassailable authority of constitutional command. Its cosmic commands come not from clay-footed legislators but from the priesthood of the judiciary.

It is certain that Irving Brant would agree with this statement, especially the "priesthood of the judiciary" phrase, but what would Thomas Jefferson and Andrew Jackson have thought of decisions of the Supreme Court referred to as "cosmic commands" of "unassailable authority;" and how would Webster, Clay and Calhoun of an earlier day, and Robert Taft, Harry Byrd and Richard Russell of more recent times, have reacted to the description of themselves as "clay-footed legislators" lacking the religious and ethical, as well as constitutional, insights of our infallible Supreme Court judges?

A New York City municipal judge has written that a "golden thread" tying together the Warren Court rulings was the belief that the Court "had the responsibility for acting when the other branches of government had not moved to correct basic inequities in the American democracy." (Judge Sidney H. Asch, *Civil Rights & Responsibilities Under the Constitution,* Arco, 1970.) Here the judge charges the Court with a duty to act in causes so compelling as to be subject to a higher law than the Constitution. It must be a higher law because the Constitution does not authorize the judiciary to correct basic inequities in American democracy—that is the duty of our federal and state legislatures, elected by the people and acting in accordance with rules laid down in our basic charter.

What are "basic inequities" and where would Judge Asch draw the line in defining the sacred duty of the Court to correct them? Are there any limits on the Court's power to identify basic inequities that require correction? Is not the requirement for workers to join a labor union and contribute to political causes which they oppose a basic inequity? And what has the Supreme Court done in this matter? Is not the failure to protect the lives and property of law-abiding citizens in our cities a basic inequity? Rather than attempting to correct this inequity, haven't the rulings of the Supreme Court tended to encourage criminal acts? Is not the right of Arthur Ochs Sulzberger of the New York *Times* to exert a massive influence on governmental action—far beyond that of the average citizen—a basic inequity? And should not the Court therefore find unconstitutional the free press guarantee of the First Amendment because it denies equal protection of the laws to the citizen who does not possess a powerful megaphone in the form of a newspaper? And what of the mother forced to send her small child by bus to a distant school in a potentially hostile atmosphere rather than to the more secure environment of the neighborhood school? Surely this is the most inequitable of all of the basic inequities that have followed from the *Brown* decision and subsequent federal court rulings on the public schools.

Obviously, Judge Asch would not favor Court interference in cases in which the liberty of the people is involved. The modern liberal is not really concerned with liberty; he is interested primarily in achieving the utopian goal of a form of equality that is unattainable, undesirable, and wholly unrealistic. For this the liberal would corrupt the Constitution, the courts, the legislatures, the school systems, and the whole fabric of American life.

The views of Mr. Brant, Judge Asch, and the liberal press constitute what must be termed a religious interpretation of the Constitution, in that they imply that our basic law has a transcendent meaning or quality that has been revealed to a priestly caste and to a worshipful intellectual and moral elite. This transcendent quality is especially embedded in the Bill of Rights, now defined as the first eight amendments and the Fourteenth Amendment. It is these amendments that contain the great and long-neglected moral truths pertaining to "equality," "civil rights," "human rights," and "civil liberties" which have been given form and substance by rulings of the New Deal Court and the Warren Court.

It is notable that the Ninth and Tenth Amendments of the Constitution are no longer inscribed on the sacred tablet and, in fact, have been erased for all practical purposes, although originally considered to be the *sine qua non* of the Bill of Rights by the ratifying states. This can be explained by the fact that the Ninth and Tenth Amendments were designed to protect the constitutional rights of the states and the liberties of the people as citizens of the states against the superior power of the federal government. On the other hand, the liberal purpose is to use the power of the central government to bring about a utopian, egalitarian society in which the states, if they are allowed to exist at all, will be little more than agencies for the enforcement of the dictates of the social engineers in control at the center.

And so, the liberal devotion is not really to the whole of the Bill of Rights as ratified by the states in 1791, but to a modern, truncated version. This version is satisfying to a temporary alliance of intellectuals and other minority groups, but, as these groups sometimes forget, it is subject to change as the political winds change. Judges in possession of overriding political power may suppress minorities as well as exalt them.

When the cult of Court worshippers, especially the news media, attempts to equate the deliberations of the Supreme Court with divine revelation, the alert citizen is inclined to be suspicious, especially if he is familiar with the liberal press attacks on conservatives in Congress who have criticized the Court and supported efforts to curb its powers or reverse its decisions. By laying a bludgeon upon the heads of critics who would dare disagree with the priest-interpreters, the liberal media have attempted to silence all public criticism. Their efforts differ little from the attempts earlier in the century of the Anti-Saloon League and various church groups to influence the public to believe that the prohibition amendment had divine sanction as God's chosen way to cure one of our longstanding moral and social ills.

Academic liberals, including the legal scholars, revisionist historians, political scientists, and social scientists generally, have been as intolerant as the journalists in defending the Court—all the while denying the right of conservatives to criticize its decisions. While most have not attempted to find divine authority for the Court's rulings, they have, with customary pretentiousness, found sanction for the Court's activism in the so-called social sciences, which are not sciences at all but, as practiced in America today, a mishmash of ideology. "It is one of the great intellectual superstitions of our time," wrote University of Michigan Professor Stephen

J. Tonsor in *National Review,* "that only the methods of the physical sciences can yield knowledge and certainty and that only these methods are legitimately applicable to man's experience." Professor Tonsor reminds us that whenever there is an attempt to base public policy upon formulations of the social sciences, which are too often in conflict with common sense, there are usually unforeseen side effects which often cause great harm to the political and social body.

The excursion of the Warren Court into the field of public policy, in which many of its decisions were based on the findings of social science rather than law and precedent, has brought unexpected results. Some of these results have been massive shifts of population in and out of the cities in which all involved have suffered; street crime of such magnitude as to deprive millions of the their most cherished liberty, the right to move about in reasonable safety; anarchy and bitter conflict in the public schools; and the wholesale annulment of state laws and findings of state courts by the lower federal courts, a development that Jefferson and other founding fathers would have considered to be a constitutional sin of the first magnitude.

Dean Acheson's views, quoted at the head of this chapter, of the place of the judiciary in the constitutional system, were set forth in an article in the New York *Times* published shortly after the Supreme Court decision upholding the right of the *Times* and the Washington *Post* to publish the so-called Pentagon Papers. In this article, Mr. Acheson expressed opinions that disagreed sharply with the Brant view of the liberal justices of the Supreme Court as prophets imbued with a moral vision and purpose not given to their predecessors or to other mere mortals. A liberal of impeccable credentials, but nevertheless a man of independent and often unorthodox views, Mr. Acheson portrayed the justices of the Court as men of very ordinary abilities and limited experience who were not qualified to provide answers to all sorts of political and ethical questions by turning them into judicial questions.

By extending judicial proceedings into the political and ethical fields, the justices have moved beyond their competence and their constitutional powers as well. This has been done by the Supreme Court's pretending to find in certain "sibylline phrases" of the Constitution clear and exact meanings that are read into the text and exist only in the prejudices and presumptions of the judges.

Mr. Acheson selected "equal protection of the laws" as one of the examples of sibylline phrases that have provided the underpinning for so many of the questionable decisions of the Supreme Court in recent decades. He might have added another phrase from the sacred text of the Fourteenth Amendment—"due process of law." Upon these two phrases the United States Supreme Court has erected an imperious power that overturns at will the laws of Congress and the decrees of the president. And it has reduced the state governors, state legislators, state judges, local officials, and school administrators to the status of minor functionaries of the federal courts.

Perhaps the strongest condemnation of the vain attempt of the intellectuals to shield a politicized judiciary from political attack—and that is the essence of this chapter—appeared in an unusually lucid statement of Irene Urban of Chicago in a letter published in the New York *Times* of March 11, 1972. The statement concludes:

> To the intellectuals of the 1960's the courts increasingly assumed authority not from constitutional grounds but from moral dictate. Courts were seen to transcend legal limits and were empowered with a quasi-religious, moral imperative. Judicial rulings became sacrosanct and judicial conduct unquestionable.
>
> In their mythicizing of the judiciary intellectuals lost awareness of the sources of the judiciary. The intellectuals forgot that judges are traditionally, prior to appointment, highly politicized members of the legal profession, who in fact normally reach the bench via successful political activity. And so their rulings will much more often derive

from political, not moral, inclination. In fact, the judiciary is no less fallible or corruptible than other men in government; but they can be more dangerous because they are exempt from the control of the people.

6

Fourteenth Amendment: The First Phase

> If the proposed amendments [incorporated ultimately in the Fourteenth Amendment] of the Constitution be adopted, new and enormous power will be claimed and exercised by Congress as warranted by these amendments, and the whole structure of our Government will perhaps gradually yet surely be revolutionized. And so will the judiciary.... the proposed amendments... will be used substantially to annihilate the state judiciaries.... Be assured that if this new provision be engrafted in the Constitution, it will, in time, change the entire structure and texture of our Government, and sweep away all the guaranties of safety devised and provided by our patriotic sires of the Revolution.
>   Orville H. Browning, Senator from Illinois (1861–1863) and member of President Andrew Johnson's Cabinet (1866–1869)

SENATOR ORVILLE H. BROWNING, conservative Republican and strong opponent of Radical Reconstruction, surely displayed prophetic insight when he foresaw the revolutionary evils that would flow from adoption of the Fourteenth Amendment to the Constitution. These evils would have become manifest almost immediately had not the Supreme Court of the Reconstruction period shown more wisdom than the political radicals in control of Congress. As it happened, Senator Browning's forebodings of a revolutionized governmental structure, in which the rights of the states would be virtually extinguished and the constitutional ideal of the widest possible distribution of power would be largely abandoned, were not fulfilled until nearly a century had passed.

The senator's insight failed in only one important respect. He could not foresee that the Supreme Court of a much later day, rather than Congress, would become the principal transgressor, a failure that is understandable inasmuch as Congress was specifically given the authority to enforce the amendment. To be sure, Congress has been guilty enough in its arrogant disregard of the rights of the states in these days of growing consolidation of power in the central government and the shriveling of state and local government. But the modern Supreme Court, most aggressive in its reach for power during the Warren regime, bears the major burden of guilt. The Court took the lead in this most recent degradation of state authority; Congress and the executive followed, sometimes meekly, sometimes aggressively, but never having the courage to take a stand to end the erosion not only of state powers but of their own powers as well.

The ideological structure supporting the present overriding power position of the United States Supreme Court in its relations with the state governments is no more than a revival of the political ideas of the more extreme Radical Republicans of the Reconstruction period of American history. This revival has been termed, appropriately enough, the "Second Reconstruction."

Standing out above all other accomplishments of the Radical Republicans of the Reconstruction period—with the exception, of course, of their participation in the abolition of slavery—was the adoption of the Fourteenth Amendment by the 39th Congress and its forced ratification by the states, many of which were not in the Union by act of Congress and therefore constitutionally incapable of performing this

Fourteenth Amendment: The First Phase

gravest of all constitutional duties, the amending of our basic law.

Not only were the ten non-states (driven from the Union by the congressional radicals after having been readmitted by the president) required to amend the basic law; they were forced to do so in violation of the very words of the Fourteenth Amendment which guarantees "due process of law." Even in the absence of any power in the Constitution that can order a state to vote for or reject a constitutional amendment, Congress forced the rump governments in the southern states to ratify the amendment. And, although President Andrew Johnson condemned the amendment and his secretary of state refused to issue an unqualified proclamation placing it in effect, it became effective in spite of the fact that it was not legally ratified. It has cast a long shadow and today holds a paramount place in our jurisprudence.

The controversy concerning the use, or misuse, of the Fourteenth Amendment by the New Deal and Warren Court activists in their drive for utopia revolves around two principal questions. First, what did Congress mean when it wrote into Section 1 of the amendment certain vaguely termed admonitions restraining the states from abridging the "privileges and immunities of citizens of the United States"; depriving any person of "due process of law"; or denying to any person "equal protection of the laws."

There is no doubt that the intent of the majority in the 39th Congress had been that the recently freed slaves would have citizenship and would enjoy full legal rights, something that had been denied them almost completely under slavery. It is doubtful that the Fourteenth Amendment intended to grant full political rights because a subsequent amendment, the Fifteenth, was found necessary in order to insure that the right of the former slaves to vote "shall not be denied or abridged by the United States or by any State on account of race, color, or previous condition of servitude." Only a handful of radicals in Congress believed that the purpose of the amendment was to promote what Russell Kirk has called "compulsory congregation" of the races in schools or elsewhere, or to insure complete equality in race relations, private as well as public, social as well as legal and political. This latter interpretation has been adopted by the Supreme Court in recent years and accepted by the executive and legislative branches of the federal government.

The second major question involving the meaning of the Fourteenth Amendment may be stated simply. Did the Fourteenth Amendment make the first eight amendments of the Bill of Rights binding upon the states? An early Supreme Court decision (*Barron* v. *Baltimore,* 1833) had held that the Bill of Rights laid restraints only upon the federal government and not upon the states. This was and is a most important question, as we shall see, because it involved the transfer of massive power from the state governments to the federal courts, a transfer that took place under rulings of the New Deal and Warren Courts.

In any judicial proceeding involving the meaning of the Fourteenth Amendment and the intention of its framers, the first and most important step would be to examine the debates in the 39th Congress on the adoption of the amendment. The examination should include a study of the debates in the same Congress on the Civil Rights Bill, with which the amendment was closely related. The investigation should also be extended to the debates on ratification in the state legislatures and conventions in order to ascertain what the states understood to be the meaning and purpose of the amendment. The next obvious step would be to study the appropriate decisions of the Supreme Court that followed the adoption of the amendment in 1868.

There is much reason to believe that the New Deal and Warren Courts did not make full and proper use of any of these sources, not even the prior decisions of the Court, which they cited only to overturn and in some cases to misread. Instead, the Court of both the New Deal and Warren periods chose to use the findings of the social sciences to buttress its decisions in the *Brown* and many other controversial cases. The Court "outgrew the sociology of the nineteenth century," according to one of the revisionist historians engaged in rewriting the history of the Reconstruction period and "began to discover new meaning in the loose phrase 'equal protection of the laws.'" (Kenneth M. Stampp, *The Era of Reconstruction, 1865-1877,* Knopf, 1969.) It comes as somewhat of a surprise to find an academic supporter of the present-day activist Court referring to the sacred text of the equal protection clause as a "loose phrase." That is exactly what it is, of course. Dean Acheson found a better term when he called it a "sibylline phrase."

The extent to which the Warren Court made use of the debates on the Fourteenth Amendment and the Civil Rights Bill has been discussed in Chapter 2. Dr. Alfred H. Kelly of Wayne State University, who was hired by the NAACP legal staff to prepare a paper on the intentions of the framers in the 39th Congress, found little to support the NAACP plea in the *Brown* decision on segregated schools. But he took that little, which amounted to the opinions of a few of the more extreme Radical Republicans, and presented these as the opinions of the majority, thus attempting to distort the record, an action which he believed was justified by the holiness of the cause.

In the debate on the Fourteenth Amendment, two of the Radical extremists stand out. One of the more vindictive, Senator Jacob M. Howard of Michigan, a native of Vermont, has been described by his biographer in the *Dictionary of American Biography* as a man who strongly opposed Lincoln's humane plan of reconstruction and favored "extreme punishment for the South." Senator Howard also favored the unlimited use of federal power in an effort to turn into reality the utopian dream of complete equality of the races in all areas of American life. It is certain that such an attempt would have meant the destruction of many of the most cherished civil liberties of the American people, North as well as South.

Senator Howard's counterpart in the House, Congressman John A. Bingham of Ohio, the principal author of Section 1 of the Fourteenth Amendment, has been described in the same biographical publication as "a clever and forceful speaker, overflowing with invective, rhetorical phrases, and historical allusions of varying degrees of accuracy." An insight into Congressman Bingham's character is revealed in his part in the military trial of the murderers of President Abraham Lincoln. Bingham was made a special judge advocate in this trial for the primary purpose of bullying the defense witnesses. He declared Jefferson Davis to be equally guilty with John Wilkes Booth in the murder conspiracy and in his summary claimed nearly unlimited extra-constitutional powers for the executive, even the power to "string up the culprits without any court." Justice Hugo L. Black, in a dissenting opinion in the *Adamson* case (1947), cited the arguments of Bingham in the debates on the Fourteenth Amendment as his principal authority for the most extreme claims ever made by a Supreme Court member as to the all-encompassing scope of this amendment.

The first Supreme Court test of the Fourteenth Amendment came in the *Slaughterhouse Cases* decided in 1873. Members of a butchers association in New Orleans brought suit in federal court, after losing in the state courts, against the state of Louisiana, claiming that a Louisiana law centralizing the butchering of livestock in New Orleans and a large surrounding area was in violation of the Fourteenth Amendment. This law, they argued, abridged their privileges and immunities as citizens of the United States, deprived them of property without due process of law, and denied them equal protection of the laws.

Whether or not the Louisiana law damaged the interests of the plaintiffs, it was legally no more than an attempt to protect the public health and, at the same time, to accord the citizens of the New Orleans area the civil rights to enjoy an unpolluted environment and an uncontaminated meat supply. The Supreme Court upheld the Louisiana law and in doing so made a distinction between rights that were derived from state citizenship and those that were derived from citizenship of the United States. The Court ruled that the Fourteenth Amendment was concerned only with those rights derived from citizenship of the United States and did not intend to transfer to the federal government the protection of the great body of civil rights, but that "almost the entire domain of the privileges and immunities of citizens of the States . . . lay within the constitutional and legislative power of the States, and without that of the Federal Government."

Some liberal historians have claimed that this great decision "slaughtered" the Fourteenth Amendment. But it preserved, for two-thirds of a century at least, the balance of federal and state powers laid down in the Constitution; and it determined for the same period of time that the state governments would not become mere appendages of the central government, as would have happened had the Court upheld the radical view of federal omnipotence in the civil rights field. Justice Samuel F. Miller of Iowa, who wrote the *Slaughterhouse* opinion, suggested that had the Court ruled against the state of Louisiana the effect would have been "to fetter and degrade the State governments by subjecting them to the control of Congress, in the exercise of powers heretofore universally conceded to them of the most ordinary and fundamental character. . . ."

The next important Supreme Court decision involving civil rights guarantees in the Fourteenth Amendment came in the *Civil Rights Cases* in 1883. Eight years earlier, in the Civil Rights Act of 1875, Congress had attempted to force equality into private business relations by declaring that the accommodations of inns, theaters, transportation companies, and similar businesses must be open to all without discrimination. When some Negroes were refused accommodations, they brought suit in federal court, claiming that they had been denied equal protection of the laws guaranteed in the Fourteenth Amendment and made enforceable by federal statute in the 1875 law. The Supreme Court ruled against the plaintiffs and held that the Fourteenth Amendment was a restraint upon the states and not upon private individuals.

The famous *Plessy* v. *Ferguson* case (1896) involved the plea of a Negro that a Louisiana law requiring separate railway accommodations for white and colored passengers was in violation of both the Thirteenth Amendment, which abolished slavery, and the Fourteenth Amendment, which requires equal protection of the laws for all citizens. The underlying question in this case was: How far does the Fourteenth Amendment go in requiring "equal protection of the laws"?

In the seven-to-one *Plessy* decision, the Supreme Court attempted to apply a rule of reason to the effect that while the Constitution requires absolute equality before the law, this is a political equality, not a social equality. In determining the reasonableness of this and similar laws, the Court is required to consider established usages, customs, and traditions, as well as the duty of the states to preserve public peace and good order. The Constitution does not require forced social equality of the races; if the civil and political rights of the races are equal, that is sufficient. Therefore, separate railroad cars for whites and colored are within the law if the accommodations are equal. The "separate but equal" doctrine held firm for nearly sixty years, or until it was overturned in 1954 by the Warren Court in the *Brown* decision.

7

Fourteenth Amendment Transfigured

> Raised up by a virtual *coup d'etat*, a century ago, the Fourteenth Amendment has become a "proud tower," like Edgar Allan Poe's, from which the Supreme Court "gigantically looks down" upon our frantic little scurryings.
>   Professor Donald Davidson, Vanderbilt
>   University (1968)

WHILE THE FOURTEENTH AMENDMENT lay dormant during the early years of this century, there were forces at work that would one day revive it and give it a place of importance in our jurisprudence never before approached. Outstanding among these forces was a rising class of intellectuals pouring out of the college and university undergraduate departments into the graduate schools, law schools, university faculties, college and secondary school faculties, communications media, labor movement, churches, and, beginning with the New Deal period of the 1930s, the federal and state bureaucracies. Under the New Deal, the intellectuals acquired for the first time in American history a strong political power base which rested not so much on their own numbers as upon their ability to influence the middle and working classes bitterly disillusioned by the postwar collapse of Wilsonian idealism in the 1920s and even more by the traumatic experiences of the great depression of the 1930s. The American people, suddenly losing much of that youthful exuberance so characteristic of their earlier history, and no longer buoyed up with childlike optimism and belief in uninterrupted progress, were ripe for exploitation by a new political aristocracy proclaiming a socialistic utopia while couching its promises in the familiar terms of the American political experience. The new aristocrats were the intellectuals who formed the vanguard of modern liberalism as we know it in American politics today.

A great number and variety of political organizations, ranging from the Communist party on the left to the Democratic party on the right, with many liberal and Communist-front groups in between, served as vehicles of the intellectual class in its rise to power at the head of the liberal-left movement. The Democratic party has been the primary vehicle, starting with Roosevelt's first term in 1933. The intellectuals formed one of the elements in the Roosevelt coalition, which included also northern and western white ethnic groups, mostly urban and Catholic or Jewish, southern whites, Negroes, organized labor, farmers, and, not to be overlooked, the limousine liberals, exemplified by the members of the Democratic wing of the Roosevelt family. In time, the intellectuals came to dominate this coalition because they made themselves the keepers of the sacred tablets, the dispensers of approved ideology, and the shapers of the party image oozing benevolence and brotherly love. After the Democratic Convention of 1948, they were able to strengthen their hold on the national party by purging its rolls of unbelievers, such as the southern white conservatives, and snubbing the farmers who had been a mainstay of the party for most of its history but who had lost much of their former political strength.

As its strength grew after the First World War, the intellectual class—allied with or acting through assorted liberal groups such as the American Civil Liberties Union, National Association for the Advancement of Colored People, American Jewish Congress, academic social science organizations, and numerous Communist-front groups—brought increasing pressure to bear upon the Supreme Court to cast aside the restricted rulings of the Court on the Fourteenth Amendment since 1873. They urged the Court to go back—to turn the clock back, so to speak—to the more extreme views of the Radical Republicans of the 39th Congress. The Supreme Court docket of the 1920s became crowded with cases involving pleas of radicals charged with violating the espionage and draft laws and other war and postwar security measures, and with cases of aggrieved Negroes attacking alleged discriminatory state laws, all invoking the "due process" or "equal protection" clause of the Fourteenth Amendment. Justice Oliver Wendell Holmes, who was to become in time an Olympian hero of the liberal-left, vigorously protested in one case the attempts of pressure groups to use the Fourteenth Amendment as a weapon for degrading the powers of the states. In *Baldwin* v. *Missouri* (1930), Justice Holmes wrote:

> I have not adequately expressed the more than anxiety that I feel at the ever-increasing scope given to the Fourteenth Amendment in cutting down what I believe to be the constitutional rights of the States. As the decisions now stand, I hardly see any limit but the sky to the invalidating of these rights if they happen to strike a majority of this Court as for any reason desirable. I cannot believe that the Amendment was intended to give us *carte blanche* to embody our economic or moral beliefs in its prohibitions.

With the coming of the New Deal in 1933, "civil rights" and "civil liberties" groups continued their legal assault upon the Supreme Court with increasing zeal; the assault included the lower federal courts and the state courts as well. And yet, few responsible voices were raised against this ancient judicial sin of barratry, "the practice of exciting and encouraging or maintaining lawsuits or quarrels: the persistent incitement of litigation." The opportunity for a break-through in their litigation efforts came at the beginning of Roosevelt's second term when Supreme Court vacancies began to occur and were filled by New Dealers strongly influenced by the activist philosophy of the eastern law schools and politically committed to the "civil rights" cause. Between 1937 and 1941, Roosevelt was able to fill seven of the nine seats on the Court, and all but one appointee, who remained a member for only a short time, were of the liberal faith. Roosevelt had packed the Court with men of his own views; and some of his appointees would remain through the turbulent Warren period and even into the 1970s.

Most revolutions begin not with violence but with reasonable demands which, when granted, are quickly escalated. The great French Revolution, probably the most important political event of modern times, began with the modest demand that the king call the Estates General into session. When the king complied in 1789, not even the most ardent revolutionist could have foreseen that within four years many ancient French monarchical institutions would be demolished, King Louis XVI and Queen Marie Antoinette would be executed, and France would be in the grip of the Reign of Terror presided over by a sanctimonious ideologue, Robespierre, who ruled by the guillotine while proclaiming devotion to liberty, equality, and fraternity.

On a much more modest scale, the Warren Revolution (or at least that phase of it called by some the Second Reconstruction) began with a very reasonable demand—that Lloyd Gaines, a Negro citizen of Missouri, be allowed to enter the all-white law school of the University of Missouri. Missouri's state university for Negroes, Lincoln University, did not have a law school at the time, but the state offered to pay Gaines's tuition at any one of the several nearby state university law schools pending the full development of Lincoln University to the level of the University of Missouri. Mr. Gaines brought suit in federal court, claiming that the curators of the University of Missouri, in refusing his request for admission to the all-white law school, had denied him equal protection of the laws guaranteed by the Fourteenth Amendment. When the *Gaines* case reached the Supreme Court, the justices, by a seven-to-two vote, held for the plaintiff by declaring that the state of Missouri must either admit Gaines to the white law school or furnish within its borders facilities for a legal education substantially equal to those at the state university law school, even though Gaines was the only Negro who wanted to study there.

However fair and just it may have seemed to the liberal mind, the *Gaines* decision opened a door that led to a revolutionary shift of power from the elected state governments to the appointed federal courts, to the *Brown* decision of 1954, the busing madness of the 1970s, and the degradation of scholarly standards for both students and teachers in all government-supported colleges and universities. *Gaines* was the first case in American history in which the Supreme Court, by applying the "separate but equal" doctrine to the schools, infringed upon the right of the states under the Tenth Amendment to run their own school systems without interference from the federal government. It will be recalled that the *Plessy* decision of 1896 made the "separate but equal" doctrine applicable only to railroad facilities. When, three years later in the *Cumming* case, Negro plaintiffs attempted to obtain a Court ruling applying "separate but equal" to schools, their plea was rejected. In the important *Gong Lum v. Rice* case (1927), the Court decided, once and for all it thought, that the Tenth Amendment reserves to the states the right to run their own school systems. Specifically, the Court ruled that the state of Mississippi had the constitutional authority to assign pupils to the schools as it pleased.

After the *Gaines* decision, it was inevitable that the Supreme Court would enlarge its assumed authority to regulate the school systems in the states under the "equal protection" clause of the Fourteenth Amendment. The nettle had been grasped and in time the *Gaines* principle was applied to the University of Oklahoma law school and graduate school of education and to the University of Texas law school. In the latter case, the state of Texas maintained a law school for Negroes at Texas Southern University, but the Court said in the *Sweatt* v. *Painter* case (1950) that the all-Negro law school was not equal to the all-white school and therefore the white school must be opened to Negro applicants. These decisions had the effect of opening all state-supported graduate and professional schools to Negroes.

It should be kept in mind that as late as 1950, in the *Sweatt* case, the Supreme Court still held to the view that segregation of the races in the public schools was altogether constitutional and was not in violation of the Fourteenth Amendment. The Court said merely that if a state chose to maintain separate schools for whites and blacks, they must be equal. The equal requirement resulted from the Court having changed its mind between the *Gong Lum* decision in 1927 and the *Gaines* decree in 1938. Four years after the *Sweatt* case, in the revolutionary *Brown* decision, the Court again changed its mind and threw the "separate but equal" doctrine out the window by holding that separate educational facilities for the races are "inherently unequal," and therefore made unconstitutional by the battered Fourteenth Amendment.

One of the frightening facts about the Warren Court experience was the frivolous, devil-may-care attitude with which the justices could approach the Constitution without fear of punishment by the American people or other retribution. The Court was wholly contemptuous of the ancient legal rule of *stare decisis,* that is, to abide by rules and principles laid down in previous decisions. The Court ran roughshod over the constitutional rights clearly reserved to the state governments and consistently upheld by earlier courts. It changed its mind at will without regard to the deeply felt interests of a very large segment of the population. Even if it be assumed that the Court's decisions were constitutionally correct, the state officials and school administrators in the affected states had the right to expect some degree of consistency so that they could maintain order in a clearly volatile, even revolutionary situation. But none of the Warren Court decisions on the public schools, including the *Brown* decision, was allowed to stand firm as the law of the land.

Soon after the *Brown* decision, the Fourth Circuit Court of Appeals handed down a decision, which the Supreme Court did not overturn, that the *Brown* decree did not require integration of the public schools but only forbade the use of state power to impose and enforce segregation. This principle was allowed to stand a dozen years or so, or until 1968 when the Supreme Court, in the *Green* and related cases, again reversed itself and the Fourth Circuit Court of Appeals by declaring that school officials in those states in which segregation had been imposed by law must actively promote integration in order to erase the last vestiges of racial discrimination in the schools.

In the *Brown* cases, the Warren Court had forbidden the assignment of pupils by state law on the basis of race; in the *Green* cases, the Court turned the Constitution upside down by declaring that in some states race must be the overriding criterion for assignment of pupils, superior to all other factors such as place of residence, school boundaries, transportation facilities, age grouping or ability grouping. The *Green* decision led to the virtual destruction of the neighborhood schools in the South, large-scale busing of pupils across school boundaries in order to promote integration, and the threat of lower federal courts in the North to impose the same large-scale busing requirement on northern public schools for the purpose of ending segregation which a federal district judge in Detroit declared in a 1971 decision to be as violative of the Constitution as the *de jure* segregation in the South.

At the time of the *Gaines* decision in 1938, who could have foreseen the bewildering, ever-changing opinions of the federal courts regarding racial integration in the public schools over a period of three decades, at the end of which many of the nation's schools had been converted into racial cockpits and were no longer able to provide even a basic education in the midst of the anarchy that existed? There were many fearful Americans in 1938 who could see the *Brown* decision of 1954 as inevitable, but none could foresee the power-drunk judges and the busing madness of the 1960s and 1970s.

The Warren Court's bewildering rulings in the school segregation and school integration cases constituted only one phase of the Warren Revolution. In many other areas the Court reached out for state powers in the guise of interpreting the "due process" and "equal protection" clauses of the Fourteenth Amendment. In the legislative apportionment cases, for example, the Court plunged directly into the political thicket, as charged by Justice Felix Frankfurter in a dissenting opinion. In another dissenting opinion in one of the apportionment cases, it was charged that the Court had "transformed a political slogan into a constitutional absolute," avoiding all considerations of "county lines, local traditions, politics, history, and economics, so as to achieve the magic formula: one man, one vote."

The Supreme Court's theft of the right of the states to divide themselves into state legislative districts began with *Baker* v. *Carr* in which the state of Tennessee was ordered, under the "equal protection" clause of the Fourteenth Amendment, to reapportion its lower house of the state legislature into districts of equal population. This principle was applied to all of the states and in time also to the state senate districts, the latter arousing a storm of opposition in Congress and an unsuccessful attempt to reverse the decision by constitutional amendment. In 1964, in *Wesberry* v. *Sanders,* the Court forced the states to divide congressional districts on the same principle. Not satisfied with reasonable and practical interpretations of these decisions by the states, the Court, in Warren's last term, laid down the doctrinaire rule that the states must seek "precise mathematical equality" among their districts, and must "justify each variance, no matter how slight," to the federal courts. This was tyranny speaking with a loud and demanding voice as the Warren Court had been speaking for the past decade and would continue to speak as it breached the separation of powers and states-rights doctrines of the Constitution.

The Warren Court's tenderhearted concern for the downtrodden was extended to the criminal in a series of famous interlocking criminal law opinions decided on the basis of the "due process" clause of the Fourteenth Amendment and the provisions of the Fifth Amendment. These decisions began with the *Mallory* decree of 1957 in which a convicted rapist had been released because of a delay of seven and one-half hours between arrest and arraignment. The *Mallory* decision was followed by the *Gideon, Escobedo, Miranda, Douglas,* and other opinions—all of which placed handcuffs on the police and made it progressively difficult for the police to apprehend and present evidence against suspected criminals.

Further handicaps were laid on the police in a series of decisions completely rewriting the Fourth Amendment law on search and seizure. In one of these decisions, *Katz* v. *United States,* even the New Deal radical, Justice Hugo L. Black, could not abide the Court's reasoning and severely condemned his fellow activists in a dissenting opinion charging them with rewriting the Fourth Amendment and, in effect, with acting as a "continuously functioning constitutional convention." Black's dissent in this case illustrates the charge that the justices of the Warren Court have been their own worst enemies. Many of the charges in dissenting opinions equal in severity the strictures of the Court's strongest critics.

8

Fourteenth Amendment and the Bill of Rights

> The answer is plain. The Federal Government, in particular the Supreme Court, thus gains new power over the states. Whereas freedom of religious establishments, freedom of speech, of the press, and of peaceable assembly, are shielded *against* Federal power by the First Amendment, now they are to come *under* that power by the artifice of "absorbing" the substance of the First Amendment in the Fourteenth. The Constitution is turned inside out. . . .
>
> Professor Peter A. Carmichael,
> *The South and Segregation*
> (Washington, Public Affairs Press, 1965)

PROBABLY THE MOST constitutionally destructive of the novel juridical concepts underlying the activist role of the New Deal and Warren Courts was the audacious claim that the restraints laid upon Congress by the Bill of Rights had been extended and made applicable to the states by the Fourteenth Amendment. This doctrine was not original with the New Deal or Warren Courts but had been asserted as early as 1925 in a very limited way by the Supreme Court which applied it in this case *(Gitlow* v. *New York)* only to the freedom of speech and freedom of press guaranties of the First Amendment. In a 1937 decision *(Palko v. Connecticut)* the doctrine was extended further, but this assault on states' rights was not actively pressed until the Supreme Court had been packed with New Dealers. And only under the Warren regime did the Court make it a major weapon in its drive for political power at the expense of the states. The effect of this doctrine, which is in essence a further extension of the powers claimed under the Fourteenth Amendment, has been to reduce to nothingness the reserved powers of the states and of the people in those areas in which the Supreme Court has elected to assert its will.

When the Bill of Rights was submitted to and ratified by the states in 1791, it consisted of ten amendments to the Constitution. The first eight guaranteed certain individual rights against encroachment by the federal government, and the ninth and tenth reserved to the states and the people those powers not specifically delegated to the central government. Only the first of the ten amendments specifically lays a restraint on Congress; the others are more general. In the ratifying proceedings in the states in 1791, it was generally assumed that the Bill of Rights was a check only upon the powers of the federal government, and this view was upheld by the Supreme Court in *Barron v. Baltimore* (1833). In this opinion, Chief Justice John Marshall stated unequivocally, "These . . . amendments contain no expression indicating an intention to apply them to the state governments. This Court cannot so apply them."

During the debates on the Fourteenth Amendment in the 39th Congress, several Radical Republican senators and congressmen made statements that could be interpreted to mean—but only by implication—that it was the intention of Congress in approving the Fourteenth Amendment to make the first eight amendments binding upon the states. Actually, the concept that the Fourteenth Amendment "absorbed" the first eight amendments of the Bill of Rights did not become a live issue until the 1920s and was not stated fully until

Associate Justice Hugo L. Black wrote his dissenting opinion in the *Adamson* case (1947). In support of his opinion, Justice Black attached a thirty-three-page summary of the debates on the Fourteenth Amendment in the 39th Congress. His summary was of questionable validity in that it was made up largely of quotations from speeches of Congressman John A. Bingham who, at the time of the debates, was not aware of the Supreme Court decision in *Barron* v. *Baltimore* and was under the impression that the restraints of the Bill of Rights were already applicable to the states.

After the adoption of the Fourteenth Amendment, the question of the applicability of the Bill of Rights to the states again came before the Supreme Court in the case of *United States* v. *Cruikshank* in 1875. In this decision, the Court upheld the earlier *Barron* v. *Baltimore* decree by stating that the First Amendment (with which the case was primarily concerned) "was not intended to limit the powers of the State governments . . . but to operate upon the National government alone. . . ." The Court stated further that the first ten amendments "left the authority of the States just where they found it, and added nothing to the already existing powers of the United States."

In the half century that followed the *Cruikshank* decision, the Supreme Court, according to Professor Carmichael in *The South and Segregation,* "repeatedly rejected the idea that the rights secured against congressional power were now secured against state power by the Fourteenth Amendment." Surprisingly enough, the first break in the Court's consistent record came in the previously cited 1925 decision of a very conservative Court sitting during the Coolidge administration. Justice Edward T. Sanford of Tennessee wrote the decision in the case of *Gitlow* v. *New York,* approved by a seven-to-two majority. Benjamin Gitlow, then a Communist leader but later a very active anti-Communist, was convicted in a state court of violating the New York criminal anarchy statute by various activities, including advocating the use of violence in the overthrow of organized government. He appealed his case through the state courts and to the United States Supreme Court on the plea that his rights under the freedom of speech and freedom of press guarantees of the First Amendment had been denied by the state of New York. The Supreme Court rejected Gitlow's plea and added that there is no absolute right to speak or publish, that a state has the right to limit utterances inimical to the public welfare, and that the New York statute was not arbitrary or unreasonable.

Had the Court stopped there, the decision would have been altogether consistent with earlier Court decrees and with the thinking of the Court at that time, but it went further and, no doubt unwittingly, laid the foundation for a later revolutionary reconstruction of constitutional law. Justice Sanford added to the opinion the following: "For present purposes we may and do assume that freedom of speech and the press—which are protected by the First Amendment from abridgment by Congress—are among the fundamental personal rights and 'liberties' protected by the due process clause of the Fourteenth Amendment from impairment by the states."

This was all the encouragement that the intellectuals and various special interest groups, working together as a loosely knit coalition, needed in order to intensify pressures on the Supreme Court for the purpose of neutralizing the police powers of the states and, consequently, the authority of the states to control activities subversive of peace and good order within their borders. In *Near* v. *Minnesota* (1931) the Court reaffirmed the Gitlow opinion by striking down a state law against publication of any "malicious, scandalous and defamatory newspaper, magazine or other periodical" on the ground that such a law was "an infringement of the liberty of the press guaranteed by the Fourteenth Amendment."

The 1925 and 1931 decrees involved only the First Amendment. Next the Court was faced with the inevitable question of the extent to which the other amendments in the Bill of Rights were made applicable to the states by the Fourteenth Amendment. Justice Benjamin N. Cardozo, an idol of the intellectual class, attempted to solve this problem in one of the muddiest decisions in the history of the Supreme Court, characterized by spurious logic, inflated rhetoric, and oleaginous phrase. This was *Palko* v. *Connecticut,* handed down by an eight-to-one decision in 1937. Cardozo concluded that "the domain of liberty, withdrawn by the Fourteenth Amendment from encroachment by the states" (he means here that the noble Court in its interpretation of the Fourteenth Amendment has rescued the maiden liberty from the wicked states) embraces only those rights so fundamental that neither "liberty nor justice would exist if they were sacrificed." Under these and other equally vague criteria, Justice Cardozo said that the Fourteenth Amendment guarantees freedom of speech and thought, freedom of press, and the right to have counsel, against encroachment by the states; but not the right to grand-jury indictment, jury trial, immunity from self-incrimination, and the right claimed in the *Palko* case, of immunity from double jeopardy.

This decision, applying the principle of "selective absorption" by the Fourteenth Amendment, was generally accepted by the New Deal Court but was completely demolished by the Warren Court in a series of decisions in the 1950s and 1960s. Before Warren resigned in 1969, the Court had totally "absorbed" the Bill of Rights in the Fourteenth Amendment. Not only were the first eight amendments interpreted to be restraints upon the states *in toto,* but the Ninth and Tenth Amendments, placed in the Bill of Rights to protect the states and the people against federal encroachment, were virtually annulled. The states no longer possessed constitutional powers in those areas in which the Supreme Court chose to assert its will, although the states had brought the Constitution into being.

However much the liberal defenders of the Warren Court portray it as the champion of freedom, individual rights, and "civil rights," the actual results of the Court's rampant activism under the "total absorption" doctrine applied to the Fourteenth Amendment have been appalling. By diminishing to a dangerous degree the police powers of the states, the Court has encouraged numerous forms of subversive activity, criminal activities, rioting in the streets in the name of peaceable assembly, wanton destruction of life and property, an anti-religious philosophy in the schools, and the flooding of the channels of communication with the vilest of pornographic materials.

One of the Court's more questionable activities has been its futile attempts to define obscenity. It has pandered to the tastes of the intellectual sophisticates while disregarding the common-sense judgments of the majority of the people deeply concerned with the welfare and moral health of the nation's children. Two of the more extreme liberals on the Warren Court, Justices Hugo L. Black and William O. Douglas, were of the opinion that all erotic expression should be protected by the Constitution under the pagan belief that obscenity is in the mind of the beholder. Surely the depth of judicial depravity was reached when an article of Justice Douglas was published in an erotic magazine at a time when the Supreme Court was considering a number of criminal obscenity cases, including some involving the publisher of the magazine in which Douglas' article appeared.

In spite of the clear intent of the framers of the Constitution to keep the federal government out of the field of religion, the Supreme Court of the New Deal and Warren periods, by applying the "absorption" doctrine to the Bill of Rights, succeeded in extending the power of the central government over religious activities in the states. The whole purpose of the religious clauses of the First Amendment—"Congress shall make no law respecting an establishment of religion, or prohibiting the free exercise thereof"—was to prevent the federal government from interfering with religious practices in the states. At the time the Constitution was adopted, some states had their own established churches; others had abolished the established church during the Revolutionary War period. None wanted the federal government forcing conformity in any religious matters or interfering with the free exercise of religion within the states. Associate Justice Joseph Story, in his *Commentaries,* wrote as follows: "The whole power over the subject of religion is left [by the First Amendment] exclusively to the state governments to be acted upon according to their own sense of justice and the State Constitutions. . . ."

This doctrine had not been seriously questioned prior to the *Cantwell* v. *Connecticut* decision in 1940, written by Justice Owen J. Roberts who, although a Hoover appointee, had become a captive of the liberals. In the *Cantwell* case the Supreme Court for the first time extended the "absorption" doctrine to the religious freedom clauses of the First Amendment and denied the right of the state of Connecticut to exercise any degree of control over the public solicitation of funds in the name of religion. Had the justices consulted history rather than liberal ideology, they would have known that from ancient times public officials have been plagued with the problem of controlling religious fakirs who solicit funds from a gullible public. A Connecticut law forbade any person from soliciting funds for alleged religious purposes from someone not of his own sect unless a permit had been obtained from the secretary of the Public Welfare Council of the state. This official was empowered to determine, after an appraisal of the facts, whether a cause was a legitimately religious one and was required to issue or withhold a solicitation permit in accordance with his findings. This was an altogether fair and reasonable law designed to discourage fraud and to protect legitimate religious causes, as well as to preserve peace and good order in the state.

The appellants in this case, three members of the Cantwell family, belonged to the Jehovah's Witnesses sect. As such they attempted to collect funds, without a permit, from householders in a predominantly Catholic community by selling books which extolled their own religious views. These proselyters carried with them a record player with a recording that described the contents of the books and embodied a general attack on all organized religious systems as instruments of Satan and injurious to man. Furthermore, the recording singled out the Roman Catholic Church for special attack.

It is not surprising that the Catholic listeners, appalled by the effrontery, were "highly offended," as Justice Roberts admitted, and were tempted to throw the Cantwells off the street. Nevertheless, Justice Roberts, speaking for the Court, found that the Cantwells' performance was not "offensive," and that the phonograph was not shown to have disturbed residents of the street. The appellants' conduct, according to Roberts, raised no "clear and present danger to public peace and order." The Connecticut law was declared unconstitutional because: "The Fourteenth Amendment has rendered the legislatures of the states as incompetent as Congress to enact such laws."

After this decision, any scoundrel, soliciting funds in the name of religion, would be free to do so in any state without interference from state or local government. Conversely, the federal government, acting through the judicial branch, would now be able to interfere at will in religious activities in clear violation of the intention of the framers of the Constitution.

With the *Cantwell* doctrine as a precedent, it could have been predicted with some confidence that the Warren Court would sooner or later find the opportunity to carry the doctrine to the extreme. It found this opportunity in the *Engel v. Vitale* case in 1962 and the *Schempp-Murray* cases the following year. In the first case, the Court held that it was unconstitutional for New York public school children to say a simple little nondenominational prayer in the classrooms. The prayer read as follows: "Almighty God, we acknowledge our dependence upon Thee, and we beg Thy blessings upon us, our parents, our teachers, and our country." This prayer was held unconstitutional because it was composed by a state agency, the New York State Board of Regents. The Court declared its intention of keeping the government, state or national, out of the business of composing prayers under "the First Amendment's prohibition against governmental establishment of religion, as reinforced by the provisions of the Fourteenth Amendment. . . ."

Defenders of the New York school prayer decision claimed that the Court was not prohibiting school prayer as such, but a year later in the *Schempp-Murray* cases, decided together, the Court forbade worship services in public schools involving the recitation of the Lord's Prayer and the reading of the Bible, even though the Pennsylvania and Maryland laws that were under attack provided for excusing pupils who did not wish to participate.

In the majority opinion in the *Schempp-Murray* cases, written by Justice Tom C. Clark, the Supreme Court was in one of its more arrogant moods. It could not be bothered with justifying its position by presenting an historical inquiry into the "establishment of religion" clause of the First Amendment, and how these cases related to it, but merely handed down two declarations. The first stated that the Court had already decisively settled that the First Amendment, including the establishment of religion clause, had been made wholly applicable to the states by the Fourteenth Amendment; and the second dictum gave the most extreme possible interpretation to the separation of religious and governmental activities, "comprehensively forbidding any form of public aid or support for religion," a quotation he took from an earlier decision. Clark ended his opinion by giving the back of his hand to future critics by asserting that any further questioning of the "history, logic and efficacy" of the Court's position is "entirely untenable and of value only as academic exercises." The sacred Court, speaking from its marble halls on the Potomac, had placed itself above public criticism.

9

Internal Security and the Communists

> Security against foreign danger is one of the [primary] objects of civil society. It is an avowed and essential object of the American Union. . . .
> James Madison, *The Federalist,* No. 41 (1788)

ONE OF THE CONTINUING THEMES in the history of modern liberalism in this country and in the world at large is a feeling of sympathy for the Communists and the Communist philosophy. This feeling waxes and wanes; it is sometimes hidden and sometimes out in the open; it is often denied, but it is always there because the liberals know that they and the Communists, being men of the left, are ideological brothers. Methods of achieving political power may differ, but the utopian aims of the liberals and the Communists overlap to a considerable degree. Furthermore, many liberals in the United States are reformed Communists who would never admit that they had been wholly wrong (although some have done so and have become strong anti-Communist activists).

Therefore, the liberals, acting as individuals or through their various agencies such as the Americans for Democratic Action or American Civil Liberties Union, have been quick to spring to the defense of Communists charged with sedition, disloyalty, or with conspiring against the security of the United States. Government suppression of the Communists or other leftists is the one issue above all that will arouse the strongest emotions in the liberal mind; this accounts for the fierce attacks on Senator Joseph McCarthy and on the House Un-American Activities Committee (renamed the House Internal Security Committee), whose investigations have been given the name of "committeeism." Liberals deeply resent the exposure of the dark past of their ideological brethren of the Left.

Beginning with the *Pennsylvania* v. *Nelson* case of 1956, the Warren Court exhibited a continuing softness toward Communists and communism in decision after decision which, taken together, greatly weakened our internal security system against espionage, sabotage, and other forms of subversive activity. *Pennsylvania* v. *Nelson,* wrote James Burnham in *National Review,* was "simultaneously a blow at states' rights, an encroachment on the legislature and a setback to domestic security." The case involved Steve Nelson, a notorious Communist who, while living in California in 1943, had passed atomic bomb secrets from scientist Joseph Weinberg to a Soviet consular officer in San Francisco. Nelson was later transferred to a Communist party post in Pennsylvania; in 1952 he was convicted of violating the Pennsylvania Sedition Act. In 1953 he was also convicted in federal court of violating the Smith Act, a federal sedition law passed in 1940 on the eve of American entrance into World War II.

In Nelson's defense, in the state courts and later in the federal courts, his attorneys presented a plea that Congress, in passing the Smith Act in 1940, had intended to occupy the internal security field exclusively and that therefore the state sedition laws were null and void. If this reading of the Smith Act were accepted by higher courts of appeal, upsetting Nelson's convictions in the lower courts, the Communists of the country would gain a tremendous advantage in being freed of prosecution in the state courts. When the appeals reached the Pennsylvania Supreme Court and the United States Supreme Court, the defense plea was accepted, and Nelson's convictions in the lower state and federal courts were overturned. The Warren Court's written opinion in this case was so loaded with error and spurious logic that L. Brent Bozell in *The Warren Revolution* has called it "one of the most astonishing analyses in the history of the Supreme Court."

The Warren Court held, with false assumptions and bad logic, that "the conclusion is inescapable that Congress has intended to occupy the field of sedition" to the exclusion of the states. Representative Howard W. Smith of Virginia, author of the Smith Act, was astonished to hear of the Nelson defense plea. While the case was still in the Pennsylvania courts, Smith wrote a letter to the attorney general of Pennsylvania in which he stated that he had had no intimation during the preparation of the act, the hearings before the judiciary committee, or the debates in the House, that Congress had the slightest intention of nullifying state sedition laws. This letter from Representative Smith was available to the Warren Court, but the Court ignored it. Within a year after the Supreme Court cleared Nelson of the Pennsylvania charge, he was also freed of prosecution under the federal sedition law, the Smith Act, on a minor technicality.

After *Pennsylvania* v. *Nelson*, it was not difficult for the Warren Court to extend its protection of the Communist conspiracy and to place it beyond the reach of state and federal law. The Court accepted in time the Black-Douglas-Frankfurter theory that the Communists were not conspirators but were members of a legitimate political party who were being punished for their political views. Because the Communists claimed to be victims of an oppressive government, the Warren Court made them a special object of its benevolence. The Court had ceased to be a dispenser of justice under the rules laid down in the Constitution. Having substituted emotion for reason, it had determined to assume a humanitarian function described by liberal journalist Walter Lippmann, in one of his more unctious moods, "to redress grievances and raise the standard of public righteousness."

American Communists and their liberal friends had much to gloat about on June 17, 1957, a decision day of the United States Supreme Court ending the Court's 1956-1957 term. A flood of decisions out of the Court's hopper on this day contained four decrees confirming the Court's benevolent concern for Communist conspirators as originally established beyond question in the *Nelson* case. Two of these decrees are of unusual importance and are very good examples of the extremes to which the Warren Court was willing to go. These are the *Watkins* decision and the California Communist cases. It should be emphasized that these were only two of many such decisions over the years in which the Warren Court, following the *Nelson* decision, threw its mantle of protection over the Communist conspiracy.

In the *Watkins* case the Supreme Court reversed the conviction of John T. Watkins, an Illinois labor leader, for contempt of Congress in refusing to answer certain questions of the House Un-American Activities Committee. In this decision, the Court rode down the right of Congress to investigate freely, pressed the investigative right into the narrow limits of legislative intent, and surrounded witnesses before congressional committees with a wall of immunity which permitted them to thumb their noses at Congress if they did not wish to testify. The *Watkins* decision, written by Warren himself, held that the legislative purpose behind the questioning of Watkins had not been disclosed to him with "indisputable clarity" and belittled Congress by implying that one of its agencies was attempting "to expose for the sake of exposure."

The *Watkins* decision was a serious interference with the duty of Congress to inform itself, as well as the people, through the investigative process. Woodrow Wilson, in his book *Congressional Government,* wrote that "the informing function of Congress should be preferred even to its legislative function." Historically, the liberals had strongly upheld the congressional right to free inquiry, especially when reluctant witnesses had been businessmen or non-liberal politicians. In "Hands Off the Investigations," a 1924 article on the Teapot Dome scandals in the *New Republic,* Felix Frankfurter, then a professor of law at Harvard, had gone to bat for the the right of Congress to investigate. Quoting Wilson in the work cited above, Frankfurter upheld the power of congressional investigations as "an effective instrument for ventilating issues for the information of Congress and of the public"; he warned against "the grave risks of fettering free congressional inquiry . . . by artificial and technical limitations. . . ." When Frankfurter as an associate justice concurred in the *Watkins* decision, he was reminded of his 1924 article by Associate Justice Tom C. Clark in the latter's dissenting opinion.

Justice Hugo L. Black had also earlier upheld the congressional right of free inquiry in a 1936 article in *Harper's* magazine entitled "Inside a Senate Investigation." Black, then a United States senator from Alabama and chairman of a Senate committee investigating utility holding company practices, militantly upheld the right of his committee to penetrate the "special privilege of secrecy" claimed by witnesses. He wrote in this article (also cited by Justice Clark in his dissenting opinion):

> There is no power on earth that can tear away the veil behind which powerful and audacious and unscrupulous groups operate save the sovereign legislative power armed with the right of subpoena and search. . . .
>
> This controversy has brought forth many legal arguments, filled many pages of parliamentary records, evoked multitudinous editorial protests, and sent many recalcitrants to prison. Notwithstanding this continuous opposition, the House and Senate have uniformly sus-

tained the right of their committees to obtain such evidence since the first congressional investigation was ordered by the House in 1792. The courts have upheld them. . . .

Apparently, Black had undergone a sea change between 1936 and 1957. In concurring in the *Watkins* decision, it is evident that he did not consider Communist agents to be members of "powerful and audacious and unscrupulous groups."

Chief Justice Earl Warren, filled with concern for the Communists in the *Watkins* and many other Supreme Court decisions, had not always felt that way. As attorney general of California in 1941, Warren was publicly outraged by a decision of the California Prison Board of Terms and Paroles, dominated by left-wing Democrats, to release from prison three Communist murderers who had served only a little more than four years of twenty-year sentences. Warren, who as district attorney of Alameda County had sent these men to prison, expressed his opinion in a newspaper statement: "Human life has indeed been cheapened. The murderers are free today not because they are rehabilitated criminals but because they are politically powerful Communistic radicals. Their parole is a culmination of a sinister program of subversive politics, attempted bribery, terrorism and intimidation which has evidenced itself in so many ways during the past three years."

In the Supreme Court decision of 1957, was Watkins released because he was a "politically powerful Communistic radical"? It was so charged by many critics of Warren and the Warren Court.

In the California Communist cases, the Supreme Court proved the truth of the ironical remark of onetime Chief Justice Charles Evans Hughes that "the law is what the judges say it is." This decision virtually destroyed the efficacy of the Smith Act (the federal sedition law) as a means of countering Communist conspiratorial activities in the country. This was done by distorting out of recognition the meaning of the word "organize" as it was used in the Smith Act.

The Smith Act prohibited the organization of all Communist party units, agencies, and fronts engaged in subversive activities. But the Supreme Court confined the meaning of "organize" to a Communist party action that took place in 1945 (this was actually a reorganization that took place at the end of the war, following a period of wartime cooperation by the party). Because the word "organize" applied only to the 1945 action, according to the decision, and five of the defendants were not indicted until 1951, the Court freed the five under the three-year statute of limitations. A new trial was ordered for the nine others who were freed on the ground of insufficient evidence. In the case of this group, Justice Tom C. Clark, in a dissenting opinion, accused the Court of usurping the function of the jury. Apparently, the liberal majority on the Court was determined to free all of the defendants by one means or another.

Nature's first law, self-preservation, applies to nations as well as persons, but this was not the view of the Warren Court. In many other decisions in the area of internal security, the Court forced defense plants and school boards to employ suspected Communists, forced state bar associations to admit individuals who refused to testify as to their membership in the Communist party, made it virtually impossible to employ FBI testimony in conspiracy cases, and removed nearly all restraints on the right of Communists to advocate the overthrow of the government by force. After these decisions, restraints on the Communists or other conspirators of the Left would be possible only if they were caught bomb in hand on the barricades. A Pennsylvania state judge, warning against the Warren Court leniency, wrote that "the member of a Communist-action group cannot be kept off an American warship unless he openly brandishes the auger with which he intends to sink the ship."

10

Intellectuals and the Court

> These are the only men professing to know how to do us good, yet they differ so much from the rest they not only do not help us as the others do, when one puts oneself into their hands, but on the contrary corrupt us.
>
> Socrates on the Sophists (399 B.C.)
>
> The true philosopher is the law-giver of society; the sophist is the false prophet who corrupts the souls of its citizens and on an empirical level destroys the just order of society.
>
> But here we are faced with a terrible irony; the very men who would have been designated sophists or "philodoxers" by Plato and Aristotle are today considered as philosophers.
>
> Peter Stanlis, *Modern Age* (1959)

WHY WOULD THE SUPREME COURT, after nearly a century and a half of reasonable restraint, and possessed of neither the power of the sword nor the power of the purse, suddenly attain, with only feeble opposition, the dominant power which it now wields? There are many reasons for this, but the principal reason is that the Court made itself the ally and agent of a politically powerful intellectual class which did not exist prior to the New Deal period. The intellectuals serve as the cutting edge of the modern liberal movement which—in contrast to the nineteenth-century liberalism of maximum liberty, free trade, and limited government—is authoritarian and statist with a primary interest of shaping mass society by governmental action to fit the latest liberal concept of an egalitarian utopia. Our Supreme Court today is very much involved in this shaping process.

Unrestrained judicial activism is the brainchild of our modern intellectuals of the liberal left. Since the Franklin D. Roosevelt administration, in which the political power of the intellectual class was firmly established, this group has extended its influence over a large segment of the various forms of public communication, the schools and universities, the labor unions, churches, federal and state bureaucracies, the foundations, newer ethnic groups, the blacks, and the more politically active segment of the student population. While the voting strength concentrated in these groups is substantial, most of the political power of the intellectuals rests upon their ability to influence the politically passive, uncommitted majority by dominance of the public channels of communication.

As it is presently used, the term "intellectuals" is a misnomer in that most of the individuals who fall within the group do not belong to our true intellectual leadership. They are not intellectuals in the classical sense, because their intellectual life is primarily utopian, projected into the future, and does not rest upon the great Western tradition of the past three thousand years. They have a shallow and distorted view of the nature of man and have little interest in religion, science, or philosophy. Most of our intellectuals are narrowly educated specialists and usually competent in a very restricted field. They certainly do not fall within Plato's definition of an educated man as one who can "see things as they are." They are, in fact, heirs of the ancient sophists, the ersatz intellectuals of the classical age; like the sophists, they constitute a rootless, undisciplined, and irresponsible element in the social and political order.

It is impossible to understand the intellectuals of today until it is realized that their primary interests are political rather than intellectual. The point was made clear in a 1969 article in *Commentary* magazine on Jewish intellectuals, whose political interests absorb a considerable share of the intellectual energies they possess. This is true of other groups of intellectuals as well. To a large extent the so-called intellectuals of today are little more than low-level brain workers with a strong taste for political power. The value that society places on their services is reflected in their generally modest incomes, although some of the shrewder and more talented have amassed fortunes. Intellectually and economically, they are below the level of the general membership of professions such as law, medicine, engineering, and the physical sciences, which require stricter intellectual discipline and greater competence. Because society does not accord the intellectuals the income, prestige, and position which they believe their abilities warrant, they tend to become rebellious and to align themselves with and give political leadership to other dissatisfied groups in society. While identifying their interests with the proletariat, they nevertheless fancy themselves an elite.

Intellectuals are found within other political groups, but the liberal creed with its utopian outlook has attracted the overwhelming majority. Because of their radical tendencies, their distorted view of human nature, their contempt for tradition and order, and their fierce and unending drive for power, the liberal intellectuals have become a menace to internal peace and an ordered society in the United States. They loudly proclaim their democratic virtues while seeking to destroy the democratic processes. With great force and persuasion they defend the arbitrary and almost unlimited rule of a small group of non-elected federal judges, while denying to Congress the right to legislate on the powers of the Supreme Court as provided for in the Constitution.

The liberal intellectual concept of the very broad powers of the Supreme Court and the limited powers of Congress has been most clearly revealed in the editorial pages of the New York *Times,* Washington *Post,* and other liberal newspapers in recent years, especially in those periods when Congress was considering legislation to limit the Court's jurisdiction or reverse its decisions. The screams of the liberal press have been deafening. "The spectacle of Congress," cried the Washington *Post* in one editorial, "trying to use its legislative power to deny or temporarily nullify constitutional rights which the Supreme Court has clearly upheld is such a serious encroachment upon the orderly division of powers that even extraordinary [revolutionary?] measures would be justified to defeat it." It is not the function of Congress, said the *Post,* to set aside the "law of the land," although, as the *Post* editor well knew, the Constitution clearly gives Congress the right to limit the Court's powers.

In spite of the tolerance shown in disorders in the cities and on the campuses, the American people have made clear that they will never stand by and see their constitutional system destroyed outright by the Communists and other extreme revolutionaries as has happened in eastern Europe, China, and Cuba. But they have watched the Supreme Court, driven on by pressures from the intellectuals, attempt to dismantle our system step by step without raising their voices, except for conservatives, especially those in the southern states where opposition to judicial rule has been strong. Unless the people of the United States can reverse the trend, constitutionalism in this country as we have known it since 1789 may well end, and with a whimper rather than a bang. It is approaching the end now for the writ of the Supreme Court runs where it pleases, and there is no existing force capable of keeping it in bounds.

All of the modern utopian "isms," whether liberalism, Rousseau's romanticism, Marxist communism, Fabian socialism, fascism, or naziism, have their roots in ancient gnosticism, the deadly rival of early Christianity, to such an extent that they have been called "gnostic movements" by Professor

Eric Voegelin in his book *Science, Politics and Gnosticism* (Chicago, Henry Regnery, 1968). Professor Voegelin, undoubtedly the leading political scientist of our time, has long held the view that ancient gnosticism in its modern forms as found in the writings of Rousseau, Hegel, Marx, Comte, Freud, and others, is the beast that is destroying Western civilization. In the eighteenth century our modern gnostics became openly anti-Christian. When the Jacobin mob of the French Revolution crowned a prostitute as Goddess of Reason in Notre Dame Cathedral—one of the most profane spectacles in Western history—and proclaimed man's ability to achieve salvation on earth, gnosticism in reality if not in name was established as the religion of the Western intellectuals and the masses who follow their lead. They accepted the gnostic doctrine as updated by Rousseau that man is naturally good but has been corrupted by a wicked social order that needs to be overthrown and replaced by a new order that will give free play to man's natural benevolence. At the same time, they rejected the Christian doctrine that man is naturally sinful and must wage a personal struggle for salvation.

"Gnosticism," wrote Professor Gerhart Niemeyer of Notre Dame in a review of Professor Voegelin's book in *National Review,* "is a religion that enables people to feel equal or even superior to God, while at the same time venting their pent-up hostility against this world and human existence within it." Modern gnosticism in its various forms is a principal source of intellectual confusion in the twentieth century. It helps to explain the moral crisis of our time which provokes our judges at the highest level, spurred on by the liberal intellectuals, to take the lead in the destruction of our constitutional system in spite of their solemn oaths to support and defend it. Our federal judges have placed themselves on the same moral level of theologians who deny God, pastors who scornfully turn on their flocks in anger and contempt, teachers who join with revolutionaries in an attempt to destroy our schools, journalists who manufacture the news in support of liberal causes rather than report it, and artists and writers who cut themselves off from our great classical and Christian traditions and produce little more than ideological trash. The modern gnostics have not only tried to murder our God, but they would desecrate our temples, burn down our universities, destroy our national shrines, rewrite our history, and besmirch our heroes while attempting to raise scoundrels to the level of sainthood.

As our barbarians run amok in this second half of the twentieth century, our liberal politicians, rather than recognizing the volcano just beneath and striving to preserve public order, attempt to appease the mob by larger handouts and to stir up its passions to ever-increasing fury. In one notable instance, a group of mob-inciters was made up of the liberal majority in Congress, members of the cabinet, and certain justices of the Supreme Court, including the chief justice, applauding the president of the United States as he shouted "We shall overcome!" and other slogans of the mob before a joint session of Congress and over national television.

Modern liberalism and ancient gnosticism have many common characteristics. A basic belief of gnosticism was that man, through no fault of his own, has been cast into an alien, hostile world, which is badly organized and ordered by evil forces. Is that not what the liberals, as well as the New Left, the Communists, and the black militants, are saying today in their peculiar mixture of arrogance and self-pity?

A second belief of ancient gnosticism which has been taken over by modern liberalism and its kindred "isms" of today is that there is a means of deliverance from the wickedness of the world, once the old order has been destroyed. The means of salvation are within human capabilities and may be found in a body of knowledge *(gnosis)* possessed by an elite. This knowledge—really no more than ideology—provides a formula for converting a wretched world into a good one. As Professor Voegelin points out, this knowledge or *gnosis* of the ancients and the moderns is not grounded in science or philosophy; it amounts to no more than subjective opinion or what Plato called *doxa* to distinguish it from philosophy and from *sophos* which is true knowledge or the divine wisdom that is the attribute of God alone.

When the Warren Court needed supporting authorities in the *Brown* case, it would not cite the law of the Constitution as expounded by the Supreme Court for more than a century, including the obvious authority of the Tenth Amendment. Rather the Court turned to subjective opinion, the gnostic *gnosis* or Plato's *doxa,* in order to justify its decision. The supporting "modern authority" included the purchased opinions of a Swedish Marxist Socialist, an unpublished work by a Negro psychologist who was an employee of the NAACP, and the published works of a group of predominantly Marxist social scientists who were political advocates of the integration cause while affecting the guise of objective scholars.

In the present war between the classical-Christian tradition and modern gnosticism, the gnostic intellectual assumes the role of prophet, as Professor Voegelin explains, and deludes himself and others into thinking that he knows the meaning of history and can predict the future. In a review by Sidney Hyman of one of the works of Arthur Schlesinger, Jr., for example, it was stated that Mr. Schlesinger "takes his stand on the common frontier where history and prophecy meet. . . ." Somewhat later, Mr. Schlesinger published a history of the John F. Kennedy administration which revealed that as a historian he had become little more than a political camp follower of the Kennedy family and was certainly not a prophet or even a careful historian, especially in those areas in which the political interests of the Kennedys were involved.

As Professor Voegelin has pointed out, one of the characteristics of ancient gnosticism was belief in magic; and this is also a characteristic of modern liberalism. If one doubts that magic is a part of the liberal ideology, let him think of our intellectuals—journalists, professors, priests, artists, actors, and politicians—dancing about the persons of the Kennedys in life and their images in death, transfixed, enchanted, awed, and sanctified by their radiant personalities, their charm, their charisma, and the magic of their smiles. Most of the intellectual class view the Kennedys and other charismatic leaders of recent decades through magic spectacles.

The liberal intellectual confuses his subjective opinion with philosophy and even with the wisdom of God. He often assumes the role of the Deity as have the members of the Warren Court who have swept aside the accumulated legal wisdom of the centuries for the ideological fancies of the hour. The ancient gnostics rejected the Christian God, but in some of their texts that have survived there is the personification of the great leader who is called the Great Life or simply the Life. Symbolic expressions similar to the Great Life often appear in the rhetoric of modern liberals. The retired head of a Negro college referred in a speech to the "great souls in history," meaning, according to the news dispatch, "those who have shown concern for the man furthest down." The only "great soul" mentioned in the news dispatch was Dr. Martin Luther King, but it is very probable that the speaker also had in mind other liberal political leaders of recent decades such as Eleanor Roosevelt, who was given the title "Great Mother of the Earth" by a group of liberal women; and Earl Warren, who was virtually deified by the head of a theological seminary overcome by his "reverence" for the then chief justice.

11

Underlying "Sham Spirituality"

> [Rousseau's] emotional romanticism has been able to develop into a vast system of sham spirituality. . . .
> The Rousseauist . . . is fascinated by every form of insurgency. . . . To meet the full romantic requirement, however, the insurgent must also be tender-hearted. He must show an elementary energy in the explosion against the established order and at the same time a boundless sympathy for the victims of it. . . .
> . . . in this dehumanizing of man the rationalist has been at least as guilty as the emotionalist. If the Rousseauist hopes to find a substitute for all the restraining virtues in sympathy, the rationalist . . . hopes to find a substitute for these same virtues in some form of [governmental] machinery . . . to which our "uplifters" are so ready to resort. . . .
> Irving Babbitt, *Rousseau and Romanticism* (1919)

PROFESSOR IRVING BABBITT, late of Harvard University, spent a lifetime as teacher, philosopher, and critic attempting to stem the tide of utopian liberalism which he saw engulfing the American intellectual community. He was a classicist and conservative who believed deeply in the "permanent things" of the Western tradition. His philosophy is set forth in greatest detail in his *Rousseau and Romanticism,* first published by

Houghton Mifflin Company in 1919 and reissued by the Meridian Press, New York, in 1955. In this work Professor Babbitt was concerned with the relationship between present-day liberalism and its immediate forebears, the rationalism or scientific naturalism of Bacon, Descartes, Hobbes, and other seventeenth-century thinkers, as well as Rousseau's sentimental romanticism of the eighteenth century.

Cartesian rationalism holds that human reason, logic, and the scientific method are the primary sources of knowledge and wisdom, superior to and independent of religion, experience, tradition, authority, prescription, and intuition. The rationalist is a devotee of abstract reasoning and tends to reject as prejudice anything not subsceptible to proof in the logical and almost mathematical sense. In the social sciences his cardinal belief is that the scientific method of the physical scientists is equally applicable to the world of human relations. He has an unfailing faith in his ability to apply the accurate measuring stick of the scientist to all of the emotions, perceptions, affections and hatreds, and hopes and fears that arise from man's soul.

Rationalism has provided one of the major philosophic underpinnings of judicial activism employed as a means for achieving political and social reforms. It will be recalled that the Supreme Court decision in *Brown* v. *Board of Education* and the related school segregation cases was based primarily on what Warren called "modern authority." The authors of the sociological and psychological treatises that comprised the "modern authority" cited by Warren were rationalists who believed that the scientific method, the basic tool of the physical scientists, could also be employed in solving a deeply embedded and long-continuing problem in the American experience—the hostility and, at times, open warfare between the white and black races. The social scientists cited by Warren supported the beliefs, accepted by the Supreme Court, that there are no inherent differences between the races, that white attitudes toward the blacks are based on prejudice and emotion solely, that racial hostility is socially created and has no basis in reason or logic. The "modern authority" further claimed that there could be no threat to public order or the cause of education but only social benefits to whites and blacks from "compulsory congregation" of the races in the public schools and elsewhere. In the aftermath of the *Brown* decision, the Supreme Court, following the lead of the social scientists, found forced integration by law to be a positive good, although the Court had initially held in *Brown* that forced segregation by law was wrong.

When the justices of the Warren Court accepted the social science treatises as authorities, they in effect shifted constitutional interpretation from its ancient foundations of prescription, law, and precedent to the unstable sands of rationalism, legal sophistry, and their own personal and political prejudices. Race relations in the South and in the country at large were not as simple as the rationalists on the Warren Court and in the law schools and the political and social science faculties seemed to believe. Many years of experience since the *Brown* decree have proven this, and today there is much agonizing reappraisal on the part of the social scientists and other intellectuals, if not the judges. In 1969, Joseph Alsop, leading liberal journalist, bemoaned "the cruelly false hopes that were raised by the Supreme Court's decision desegregating the schools," and was ready to admit that "there was bad science behind the raising of those false hopes." A year earlier, Gunnar Myrdal himself, author of *An American Dilemma* cited in the *Brown* opinion, is reported to have made a speech at the City University of New York in which he confessed that he was not nearly so certain of his solutions to the racial problem as he had been twenty-five years earlier.

Scientific method as employed by our corrupted social sciences could not begin to penetrate the surface of the race relations problem and was certainly not capable of finding a solution. The inadequacies of the rationalist authorities cited by Earl Warren in the *Brown* decree are most clearly apparent in the poll of 849 social scientists, who were asked for their opinions on racial segregation in the schools. The easily anticipated replies of these social scientists were not based on true science but on subjective opinion and were no more than the rationalizing of the political opinions of a group of academic liberals who had had little or no direct experience with the race problem.

Another fallacy of the rationalists which has been accepted by the Supreme Court and its supporters is that all human problems are susceptible to solution through the agency of governmental machinery. When a social problem is of sufficient scope to become a political problem, the rationalist solution is to pass a law—or, since 1954 perhaps, to take a short cut and solve the problem by judicial decree. In the case of the liquor problem, the reformers insisted on going beyond regulatory local and state laws that reflected the views of the people at the community level to force through an amendment to the Constitution, thereby hoping to make prohibition so permanent that the liquor interests and other opponents would never be able to reverse it. This rationalist solution, which was claimed to be superior to the religious or other solutions to an ages-old problem, turned out to be such a colossal failure that the amendment was repealed within a dozen or so years. The "experiment, noble in purpose," but which became the mother of gangsterism, the speakeasy, and a scofflaw attitude toward all legal restraint, left many scars on the American psyche. Similar results can be expected from the present fierce drive toward government-enforced race mixing in the schools. The dogmatic race mixers have achieved only disruption of the schools, retardation of the educational process, and intensification of the racial war.

In the world at large, one of the continuing dogmas of the rationalists has been universalism, which holds that the evils of war and nationalism can be ended by setting up a world state to which all men would pay homage. Edmund Burke had something to say on this in his *Reflections on the Revolution in France:* "To be attached to the subdivision, to love the little platoon we belong to in society, is the first principle (the germ, as it were) of public affections. It is the first link in the series by which we proceed toward a love to our country and to mankind." The universalists, who more often than not are uprooted intellectual vagabonds not attached to any community or settled group, despise Burke's sentiment as no more than narrow provincialism. But it lies at the heart of public morality, and it embraces a true love of mankind which is not found in the universal humanitarianism of the rationalist.

Rousseau's emotional romanticism has had an even greater influence on modern liberalism than the rationalist philosophy. Professor Babbitt's fundamental quarrel with Rousseau arose from the latter's rejection of the classical and Christian concept of the duality of human nature. Rousseau denied the struggle between good and evil in the human soul and attempted to substitute another duality, an imagined struggle between good men and an evil society. This concept did not originate with Rousseau but came down through ancient gnosticism of the Roman Empire from even earlier periods of human society. Rousseau raised it to the level of a secular religion.

Rousseau's creed held that man is naturally good but has been corrupted by society. This belief leads to the modern liberal cult of pity or sympathy for the imagined victims of society, which Professor Babbitt has called "sham spirituality." The gushing sentimentality of Rousseau's romanticism, manifesting itself in modern liberalism, subordinates all of the other values of life and all of man's virtues to an unbridled sympathy—not necessarily for the real victims of society, but for momentarily fashionable favorite groups. These groups are often the less stable elements in the social order, but always susceptible to manipulation by the liberal political leadership.

Rousseauism discloses itself in an onrush of sentiment, unguided and unrestrained by intelligence, reason, principle, or sense of discrimination between true justice and special privilege. It appears in the opinions of the liberal judges of our Supreme Court and the lower courts who seem indifferent to the rights of the law-abiding majority but easily develop great sympathy for the lawbreaker. Furthermore, the liberal judge will have a special concern for some depraved criminal, student rioter, or Communist conspirator if he is a member of some favorite minority group. The more morally degraded the object of the Rousseauist's sympathy, the more spontaneous is the gushing forth of sentimental humanitarianism.

Rousseau's romanticism embodies a cult of violence as well as a cult of brotherhood. Strongly blended with the Rousseauist's sentimental streak, his sympathy for the underdog, is an innate insurgency, a rebelliousness ready to break out at any time in violence against the established order. The true Rousseauist must not only be tender-hearted; he must be ready at all times to use any means, including any form of violence, to overturn the social order if it is deemed to be oppressive. As one critic has written, the thought of Rousseau is "heavily charged with revolutionary explosives . . . it exasperates and inspires revolt and fires enthusiasm and irritates hatreds; it is the mother of violence, and source of all that is uncompromising; it launches the simple souls who give themselves up to its strange virtue upon the desperate quest of the absolute, an absolute to be realized now by anarchy and now by social despotism."

The liberals on the Warren Court and their supporters had always a special sympathy for the man of violence—the members of the mob destroying the peace and good order of the state, often in the name of non-violence, the destructive anarchists, and the Communists openly bent on destroying Western civilization and building a Marxist leviathan on its ruins. Many liberals seem fascinated by the violence of the Rousseauists of the French Revolution. Perhaps the most enthusiastic and most violent Rousseauist of them all was

Maximilien de Robespierre, the Jacobin dictator and terrorist who led in launching the Reign of Terror that held France in its grip for a year during the most turbulent period of the Revolution. While the guillotine worked feverishly under his orders and the heads of his political enemies, both real and imagined, were rolling in the streets, Robespierre was standing before the national convention proclaiming his "sublime and sacred love for humanity." In his last speech to the convention, before his own head rolled, he was perfectly sincere in defining virtue as that "tender, irresistable, imperious passion, torment and delight of magnanimous hearts, that profound horror of tyranny, that compassionate zeal for the oppressed. . . ."

In our own country today, there are many liberal intellectuals who, in the manner of Robespierre, proclaim their love for humanity and the rule of the masses while giving their political support to an all-powerful central government, including a small group of appointed justices of the Supreme Court wielding tyrannical powers seized from the other branches, the states, and the people. Among these intellectuals are the liberal clergy, many of whom have discarded Christianity for the sentimental humanitarianism, or, shall we say, the sham spirituality, of Rousseau. They now profess Christianity not as an end in itself but only as a means for achieving some form of utopian socialism. Some of them even "now see the day when clergy-led violence may be recognized as a moral means of changing social structures." At a conference on church and society sponsored by the National Council of Churches in 1967, one of the conferees stated that "violence can be expected" along with non-violent means to overthrow the present social order and bring about a "communal type of existence." The clerical proponents of violence have been given a name—they are "snipers in the steeples."

In a meeting in 1969, a committee of this same National Council of Churches condoned student violence then raging

Underlying "Sham Spirituality"

on many college campuses, in the belief that "God is in some way present in the midst of these movements, and we should be prepared to see in them his creating of a new order." An Episcopal priest saw as an "action of the Holy Spirit" the attempts of James Forman and his group of black militants to blackmail the Christian churches by invading the churches during services, taking over the national church headquarters, and threatening other acts of violence unless huge sums of money were turned over to the Forman organization.

One of the more syrupy religious affairs reporters—a fairly new and misbegotten breed of secular journalists—became quite angry in print with the "black racists" for invading the Riverside Church in New York City during morning worship. He recounted all that the Riverside Church had done to aid the black revolution and was appalled at the failure of the blacks to appreciate the support that had "flowed from the compassionate heart of a great religious fellowship." He shook his fist in print at the black intruders and proclaimed that his own response is "swift and angry: Throw the intruders out" for "they have profaned the holy with their insolence." At the end of his news dispatch he flashed his liberal credit card by taking care to assure his readers that he was as much opposed to white racism as to black racism. The reporter's angry reaction was not shared by the National Council of Churches and many of its component church groups which, in effect, condoned Forman's threat of violence and accepted his demands in principle although refusing to pay the whole of the half billion dollars demanded.

The thoughts on violence of other groups of liberals among the teachers, journalists, and politicians differ little from those of the radical clergy. It should be remembered that the leading American apostle of present-day violence, Professor Herbert Marcuse of Brandeis University and San Diego State, is a member of the teaching profession. He trained Angela Davis at Brandeis, and he has many other disciples on the faculties of the nation's colleges and universities. There are many concerned individuals on and off campus who believe that the troubles of the University of California at Berkeley stem in large part from the open and covert support that the majority of the faculty at Berkeley has given the rioting students and non-student hoodlums. Nevertheless, it should be said that at Berkeley and throughout the country, many liberal faculty members who have personally experienced violence or who fear it, and those who have been driven out of their jobs at Berkeley, Cornell, and elsewhere, are rethinking their political positions. Unfortunately, they have found that the peaceful and secure ivory tower for thinking liberal thoughts and devising utopian reform programs no longer exists. The barbarians have moved into the tower and are encamped in force in nearly all of the formerly prestigious halls of learning. Many of the professors have attempted to escape from the atmosphere of violence by moving from one campus to another, but they have found too often that they are merely jumping from the frying pan into the fire.

Some white liberal politicians, usually from outside the South but including some southerners such as Lyndon B. Johnson, Hugo L. Black, and Ramsey Clark, have had strong ideas about using violent means for advancing the interests of the blacks in the South, when in conflict with white interests, and for forcing congregation of the races in the schools and elsewhere. One senator, the late Richard L. Neuberger of Oregon, known for the purity of his liberal ideology, expressed some very clear ideas about the use of troops to enforce in the South the decrees of the Supreme Court. The senator, no doubt overcome by his sympathy for the oppressed, proposed in a public speech that a federal police force modeled after the Royal Canadian Mounties be organized and sent into the South to protect the civil rights and lives of the Negroes. He informed his liberal audience that he had been studying Canadian statutes creating the red-coated force "because this may prove to be the one way of safeguarding the Negroes of the southern states in the exercise of their inalienable rights to vote, to be equally educated, to be respected and not to be discriminated against."

Through all of the mob violence of the decade of the 1960s, whether it was instigated by militant blacks, radical students, anti-Vietnam War protesters, anti-HUAC protesters, Communists, or the New Left, the liberal press and other liberal communications media of the country generally condoned or sympathized with the violent mobsters. It is very probable that violence at the University of California at Berkeley and other universities and colleges was directly related to the 1960 attempt of a massive northern California mob, including many students from area colleges, to break up a hearing of the House Un-American Activities Committee held in San Francisco. Here the academic mob under Communist leadership tasted blood and found it good, and at the same time the members of the mob found themselves heroes in the press, on radio and television, and in the liberal community generally. The New York *Times,* Washington *Post,* and other liberal newspapers attempted to justify this violent mob action, played it down as no more than a mild demonstration of well-meaning students expressing their disapproval of "committeeism," and heaped scorn upon those conservative groups that displayed the film of the rioting as evidence of the revolutionary threat to the nation.

The reporters of the press and television networks have hovered over the racial disturbances in the South like a flock of vultures looking for carrion in the form of violent happenings and sometimes creating them to satisfy the corrupted tastes of themselves and their readers and viewers. They always express approval of the violent action of the black mob, or of federal troops or United States marshals, if employed against whites; but they quickly condemn any violent response on the part of the whites, including white police forces charged with preserving the public order. To the liberals—and much of the American press and other communications media is dominated by them—violence is to be condoned if employed to overturn the present social order, but should be condemned when employed to maintain law and order and a reasonable degree of public tranquility.

12

Earl Warren, Heroic Lawgiver

> A judge should not accept inconsistent duties; nor incur obligations, pecuniary or otherwise, which will in any way interfere or appear to interfere with his devotion to the expeditious and proper administration of his official functions.
>
> Canon 24, Canons of Judicial Ethics
> of the American Bar Association

FROM THE TIME HE ARRIVED in Washington to assume the chief justiceship in October, 1953, Earl Warren came under the influence of the Eugene Meyer family, owners and publishers of the ultra-liberal and powerful Washington *Post.* Eugene Meyer was the business head of the family; his wife Agnes was the political activist and publicist. Over the years the Meyers converted Earl Warren into their very own political lapdog. Many favors were conferred on Warren by the Meyers, and they received favors from him in return. Defenders of Warren would claim, no doubt, that the relationship with the Meyers was no more than a normal friendship between two families. But the truth is that both the Meyer family on the one hand and Earl Warren on the other occupied strong positions of power, and each was capable of conferring great benefits, involving the public weal, on the other. A closer reading of Canon 24 of the Canons of Judicial Ethics of the American Bar Association should have warned the chief justice to avoid close friendships that might compromise his independence.

Eugene Meyer came of a wealthy family of European bankers. His father, an immigrant from France, had been a partner in the banking house of Lazard Freres, first in California and later in New York. After graduating from Yale University Eugene Meyer joined his father's firm on Wall Street, but at an early age he purchased a seat on the New York Stock Exchange and struck out on his own. His greatest financial achievement was the organization of the giant Allied Chemical Corporation in 1920. The writer of one of his obituaries in the *Post* made this appear to be a great stroke of financial statesmanship, but an article in *Forbes* magazine of May 15, 1969, painted an entirely different picture. Allied Chemical was created by the merger of a group of large chemical companies; and officers of some of the companies were bitterly opposed to the consolidation. The merger was "no love affair," the *Forbes* writer stated, but was "more like a shotgun wedding." Eugene Meyer conceived the merger and his right-hand strong man, Orlando F. Weber, bulled it through. It created bitterness and resentment throughout the corporation that persisted for years and continued to have an effect into the 1960s. According to the *Forbes* article, "Allied never lived down its own history. The unresolved conflict lived on. For generations."

Eugene Meyer first came to Washington in World War I as an aide to Bernard Baruch on the War Industries Board and as chief of the War Finance Corporation. He served every president from Wilson to Truman in one financial capacity or another and developed a decided taste for life at the seat of power in Washington. On June 1, 1933, he gained for himself and his family a strong position of power in the capital city when he purchased at auction the moribund

Washington *Post* for $825,000. He had to spend $10,000,000 beyond the original purchase price, but in time he developed a most valuable property. He added radio and television stations and in 1954 purchased the Washington *Times-Herald*, his only morning rival. After Meyer's death in 1959, his heirs acquired control of *Newsweek*, the principal competitor of *Time* in the weekly popular news field.

Because of its monopoly of the morning newspaper field in Washington—where it has long been required reading for all government officials or others who have to know the latest liberal line on public questions—the *Post* owners occupy a peculiarly powerful position. The *Post* exercises its power with such ruthlessness that virtually all public expressions of opinion in the Washington area contrary to the doctrinaire liberal line are drowned out, although there is an occasional exception in other newspapers of the area.

Several years before the death of Eugene Meyer in 1959, active management of the *Post and Times-Herald,* to give its full name, had passed to one of Meyer's daughters, Katherine Graham, and her husband, Philip L. Graham; they published the paper until Philip's death in 1963. Agnes Meyer had gone into semi-retirement upon the death of her husband, but she continued for another decade to speak her mind on public questions and her activities were given full coverage in the news columns of the *Post*.

One of the secrets of the success of the Meyers in the newspaper field has been their ability to bring together a staff of able writers, well versed in the extravagant language of liberal journalism. Theirs is also the language of arrogance and insolent self-assertion, the human qualities most detested by Socrates and the ancient Greeks. The classical sense of restraint and proportion and the Christian concepts of generosity, fairness, humility, and decorum are not virtues in the Meyer ideology; they are weaknesses. Political enemies and conservatives generally, notably the white southerners for whom the liberals have a special hatred, are constantly attacked by the Meyer staff of editorialists, reporters, and cartoonists.

On the other hand, the hearts of the *Post* reporters melt with the most tearful sentimentality when reviewing a music recital of Marion Anderson long past her prime; reporting the death of a teenage black terrorist in a shootout with the police; or recording the passing of some political zombie who had never veered from the ritualistic liberal line in a lifetime of left-wing activity.

At other times, the *Post* editorialist takes off into the wild blue yonder in the most mawkish and extravagant flattery of some trained seal such as Earl Warren on his birthday, or upon the retirement of a political favorite such as Felix Frankfurter or Herbert Lehman. One of the *Post* obituaries of Eugene Meyer solemnly described him as a journalist who was determined to maintain a wall of separation between the editorial columns and the news dispatches. The obituary stated that Meyer believed that Americans "wanted their news straight, unslanted and uncolored; and reporters of the *Post* were under orders to write it that way." This is undiluted hypocrisy. The Washington *Post* under the Meyer family ownership has become notorious among modern newspapers for using its news columns to promote its editorial opinions.

When Earl Warren reached Washington in 1953, he came into a city of turmoil in which Senator Joseph McCarthy of Wisconsin had the liberals on the defensive but was unable to deliver the stroke that would have seriously diminished their influence. McCarthy looked in vain for some help from President Eisenhower, but the latter responded—unknowingly, it is true—by appointing Earl Warren as chief justice of the United States. Shortly thereafter, Senator McCarthy suffered a setback that damaged beyond repair his political standing. McCarthyism had been defeated; but Warrenism came on with a flourish, and the liberals now entered upon their years of greatest glory that were to reach a climax in the John F. Kennedy administration.

Before Earl Warren was appointed chief justice, the liberals had been in a state of frustration as to how they could gain control of the power levers that would make it possible for them to achieve their political goals more quickly than through normal constitutional processes. The liberals could not control Congress because of a coalition of northern and southern conservatives in the two major parties, and they could never quite control the Eisenhower administration. Agnes Meyer herself became so disillusioned with Eisenhower that she turned her back on the liberal Republicanism of her early years in Washington and gave enthusiastic support to the Democratic party and one of her favorite proteges, Adlai Stevenson, Eisenhower's opponent in the election of 1956.

After all the trials and tribulations of the McCarthy period, and the apparent indifference to liberal goals of the bland Eisenhower, the liberals found their spirits suddenly uplifted by the Warren Court decision in *Brown* v. *Board of Education.* Here was the key to the problem of power, the lever that would give them the means for recasting society in the liberal mold. It was the shortcut they had been striving for that would make it possible to bypass the slow-moving legislative and executive branches. It was a thrilling moment for the committed liberals. Agnes Meyer proclaimed that the *Brown* decision "could be an historic moment in history." She and her fellow liberals knew that they had scored a breakthrough, and in time they would be able to impose their collective will on the political branches and the recalcitrant state governments.

Whatever misgivings might have existed about Earl Warren's liberalism when he was first appointed to the chief justiceship vanished quickly after the *Brown* decision in May, 1954. And in decision after decision, the Warren leadership of the Supreme Court handed to the liberals many of the things they had been striving for but could not obtain through the regular political and legislative processes. Earl Warren became a hero over night, and during the next fifteen years his lofty place in the liberal pantheon was rivaled among his contemporaries only by that of Eleanor Roosevelt, Adlai Stevenson, and John F. Kennedy. The Washington *Post* editorially and in its news columns, and Agnes Meyer in her speeches, must be given a considerable share of the credit for raising Earl Warren to the level of heroic lawgiver. Other liberal papers and spokesmen were high in their praise of the new guru, but the *Post* had a monopoly of the morning newspaper field at the seat of government and was in the position to become the leading trumpeter.

From the time of the *Brown* decree until Earl Warren's retirement, the Washington *Post* took advantage of every opportunity to come out with an editorial praising Warren's virtues in the most extravagant language. The occasion might be the handing down of a new landmark decision, it might be the fifth or tenth anniversary of the *Brown* decree or the tenth anniversary of Warren's appointment, or it might be Warren's seventieth or seventy-fifth birthday. On every occasion, the *Post* threw aside all restraint in praise of Warren's "ripened understanding of human nature, human needs and the patterns of human adjustment," "his harmonious skills and his political wisdom," "his judicial statesmanship," "the blend of common sense, compassion and ardor which he brings to [the] highest judicial office," his "recognition that contemporary sociological and psychological insights forbade further reliance on the fiction of half a century that racially segregated public schools can be said to offer equal educational opportunity."

On the tenth anniversary of Warren's appointment, the *Post* proclaimed:

> It was a piece of magnificent good fortune that the Chief Justiceship was held during this trying period by a man of exceptional poise and strength and understanding. Knowing that it is the function of the Supreme Court

at times to check the popular will, Chief Justice Warren has gone about his high duties with quiet equanimity. He can be sure that in the perspective of history he will have the deep gratitude of his countrymen. We wish the country a long continuation of his superb public service.

Of course, a man of honor, humor, and self-respect would have objected strongly to this type of extravagant flattery. The *Post* editorials actually implied that there were questions in the public mind about Warren's appointment, his qualifications, and his place in history, and that these questions must be erased by shouting his praises from the rooftops. It is evident that Warren was more than willing to accept this sycophantic flattery without protest. With such lofty praise of his services, he may be forgiven if at times he suspected that he should be sitting on Mount Olympus alongside an earlier liberal idol, Justice Oliver Wendell Holmes, whom the liberals had planted there after his death.

Along with the editorial campaign in the *Post,* Agnes Meyer made frequent speeches defending the Warren Court decisions. In other speeches she pushed her favorite program—basically socialistic and very definitely anti-Christian in its concept—of "creating a new morality" through the benign operations of the public schools. What irony that she would find toward the end of her long life of supporting public schools and the "civil rights" movement that "civil rights" as proclaimed by her hero Warren and his colleagues had virtually destroyed the public school system as an educational institution in her own city of Washington. Instead of creating a new morality, the public schools in Washington and many other cities had very nearly ceased to educate and had become the lair of human predators, vandals, and rabid revolutionaries.

In one speech, Agnes Meyer expressed the fear that American society was "sinking into a cultural barbarism," and added that the only answer to the problem was to be found in her favorite institution, the public schools. She voiced her "passionate conviction that the public school system is the only institution we now possess that can serve as a lever to raise our whole culture to higher levels of creativity, whether in science or in the arts." Here was the complete rationalist and secularist speaking, one who was wholly incapable of perceiving a plane of being above that revealed in the workings of her own limited mental processes. In an earlier age, such a speech would have aroused strong indignation in many religious leaders, who would have objected to this elevation of a secular institution while virtually denying a place in our society for the church and church-related institutions. Agnes Meyer had a number of friends among the liberal clergy and no doubt they agreed with her. One of her closest clerical friends, the Reverend Duncan Howlett, pastor of All Souls' Unitarian Church in Washington, wrote a book review in which he protested against the "Christian bias" in a work on eighteenth-century philosophy.

Agnes Meyer had many of the beliefs and qualities of character of Eleanor Roosevelt, but there were some differences. Agnes was better educated, but she had much rougher manners than Eleanor, who retained some of the breeding of her upper-class heritage even though her political instincts drew her to the low road in public affairs. Agnes could wield a verbal meat axe reminiscent of Carrie Nation of the prohibition movement, who delighted in taking a real axe and wrecking the interior of any saloon she encountered in her state of Kansas.

In a 1965 speech accepting the National Brotherhood Award of the National Conference of Christians and Jews, Agnes Meyer quickly threw brotherhood out the window and took after the critics of the Warren Court with the utmost ferocity. With the head table graced by Earl Warren himself, Associate Justice William O. Douglas, Adlai Stevenson, and Secretary of Labor W. Willard Wirtz, she accused the "crackpots" and other "vociferous enemies of the Court" of "hysterical attacks," "careless abuse," "rabble-rousing nonsense," "frenzy and bigotry," and "scurrility." The attacks on the Court, she said, if tolerated, reveal a nation that "is not only lacking in culture, but is not even civilized." Furthermore, the stupid critics did not even know that the recent decisions of the Supreme Court "breathe new life into the wisdom of our forefathers." What would Thomas Jefferson have thought of that?

After the death of her husband, Agnes Meyer took upon herself the patriotic duty of providing her friend Chief Justice Warren and his wife with some of the luxuries she had known since her marriage to Eugene Meyer in 1910. Beginning at least as early as 1961, perhaps earlier, and continuing for several years thereafter, Earl Warren and his wife were the guests of Agnes Meyer on long summer cruises by chartered yacht through European waters. And on all of these cruises another pair of constant guests was none other than Drew Pearson and his wife. What a trio of political adventurers—Earl Warren, Drew Pearson, and Agnes Meyer—sailing the ocean blue together, up the Norwegian coast in 1961, up through the Adriatic in 1962 to visit Tito at his summer palace on Brioni Island, and into the Black Sea in 1963 to visit Khrushchev at his vacation villa at Gagra. They seemed strangely attracted to Communist dictators, but that is no more than a typical liberal weakness.

Sometimes there were other guests on these summer yacht trips, but always there were the Warrens and the Pearsons. A concerned citizen interested in the ways of his rulers might have asked why the man occupying the exalted position of chief justice of the United States would publicly reveal himself as the boon companion of a keyhole journalist such as Drew Pearson and a highly partisan political radical such as Agnes Meyer. Both Pearson and Agnes Meyer were powerful spokesmen for the liberal-left view, and both were quite reckless and irresponsible in their attacks on critics of the Warren Court. Rather than avoiding associations that might "incur obligations, pecuniary or otherwise," Chief Justice

Warren no doubt felt a sense of gratitude to his yachting companions and welcomed the friendship. Throughout Warren's career on the high Court, Drew Pearson followed the lead of the Washington *Post,* in which his column appeared, and never referred to the chief justice except in terms of the most extravagant and servile flattery. In the Pearson column, Earl Warren was always the heroic lawgiver.

In return for the many favors conferred by the Meyers, Earl Warren placed the power and prestige of the chief justiceship at the service of the Meyer family. On nearly every occasion when either Eugene or Agnes Meyer was honored with a public dinner, whether it was a birthday celebration, an anniversary date of Meyer's acquistion of the *Post,* or the occasion of a brotherhood or other award, Chief Justice Earl Warren sat at the head table lending the great prestige of his position to the event. These public dinners were always lavishly covered by the *Post* reporters and photographers, and on each occasion one of the photographs in the *Post* showed Earl Warren bending over the guest of honor with benign countenance and clapping hands. The Meyers were never able to attract the president to these events, and the vice president only once, but Chief Justice Earl Warren was usually there. And when Eugene Meyer died on July 17, 1959, it was Earl Warren who delivered the eulogy at a memorial service at the All Souls' Unitarian Church in Washington.

The Meyer family was able to bring to Chief Justice Earl Warren a gift which he very much desired and, in fact, needed in order to sustain his activist course in the midst of the controversies that swirled about it. This was the enthusiastic political support of the dedicated liberals who followed the *Post*'s lead in public affairs, and for whom the *Post* served as leading trumpeter at the seat of government. The Meyers, in turn, were allowed to use the prestige and exalted position of the chief justiceship as they strove to build up their image as powerful political figures, makers of public policy, cultural and social leaders, and great public benefactors.

Both Eugene Meyer and Earl Warren were hungry, ambitious seekers for power and prestige without regard to cost in honor or self-respect. For them to maintain an outward semblance of inner worth, their egos needed constant, servile flattery, the more extravagant the better. They flattered each other, and Agnes Meyer and the whole of the staff of the Washington *Post* flattered them both as they reached out for power and for that wide public esteem and respect which always seemed to elude both. Edmund Burke observed that "flattery corrupts both the receiver and the giver," and it is as true today as it was in Burke's time and at the very beginning of human society.

13

Earl Warren, Constitutional Anarchist

> It is strange, indeed, to reflect that under a Constitution which provides for a system of checks and balances and of distribution of power between national and state governments, one branch of one government—the Supreme Court—should attain the immense and, in many respects, dominant power which it now wields. We believe that the great principle of distribution of powers among the various branches of government has vitality today and is the crucial base of our democracy.
>
> Report of the Conference of State Chief Justices (1958)

THE CONSTITUTION LIES AT THE VERY HEART of our national life, and when it is violated on a massive scale over a period of years, in the guise of constitutional interpretation, our society begins to display symptoms of chaos, dissolution, and decay. Constitutional anarchy such as we have experienced since 1954 and earlier has begotten anarchy in our political, social, economic, and even religious relationships. Among the many evils, flowing directly from our present state of constitutional nihilism, are disruption in the schools, heightened racial tensions, massive dislocations of population, large-scale public disorder, and growing disrespect for the law. We are also afflicted with such side effects as licentious and unbridled behavior, foulness and lewdness in print and speech, and a general sense of permissiveness and abandon in our national life. All of these trends have accompanied the Warren Revolution.

Although the United States Supreme Court has the duty to dispense equal justice under law, many of its decisions in recent years have not served equal justice or even been lawful. Earl Warren and his fellow justices took the judicial oath that they would protect equally the rights of all; but in their decisions and in a number of their speeches, it became clear that the chief justice and his fellow activists had given up their constitutional role as impartial interpreters of the law to become partisans of those favored groups in our society which the politically powerful liberal intellectuals had selected as objects of their altruistic concern.

Earl Warren's speeches during his chief justiceship—usually contrived affairs staged by his adherents for public relations purposes—testify to his anarchical view of the place of the Supreme Court in the constitutional scheme. Perhaps more revealing than his official opinions on the bench, his public statements disclosed a man of commonplace mind and narrow prejudices, with a very shallow view of human nature and the forces that move human society. Nothing in these speeches suggested that Earl Warren was qualified to occupy the exalted position of chief justice of the United States for nearly sixteen years.

When Warren, then governor of California, was campaigning for the Republican presidential nomination in 1948, he condemned what he called the "reactionary" citizen because this particular class of human being was not concerned with "human needs." Here was one of those syrupy, meaningless terms that liberals like to throw around loosely to prove they have "heart." It was a favorite of Warren. Some years later, in defending the decisions of the Supreme Court, he attempted to justify the Court's taking over the prerogatives of the states by claiming that the states had "failed to meet the needs of the people." An editorial in the *Wall Street Journal* took him to task. "The Supreme Court has set itself up as the final arbiter," the editor wrote, "not of the law—but of the needs of the people." Was Warren really concerned with the needs of the people, or was he indulging in some of that sham spirituality so often found in liberal rhetoric?

Who is to determine the needs of the people, assuming this meaningless general term could be defined? According to Chief Justice Earl Warren, the Constitution granted this right to a handful of appointed federal judges far removed from the daily life of the people, presumably because the Supreme Court possessed a wisdom superior to that of all the state legislatures, state courts, county boards, city councils, school boards, and other state and local agencies elected by the people. The Warren Court had overturned a number of state laws concerned with subversion, religious training in the schools, strikes, inquiry powers, state employment qualifications, and standards of practice at state bars. "In none of these cases," the *Wall Street Journal* editorial added, "can it fairly or truthfully be said, as Mr. Warren did say, that the states had failed to meet the needs of the people as the elected representatives of the people determined them." The state governments had been ably and conscientiously discharging their prescribed duties in areas reserved to them by the Constitution. In undoing the work of the state legislatures and other state agencies, the Warren Court was in fact substituting its own judgment of human needs for that of the elected representatives of the people. It was constitutional anarchy masquerading as the law of the land only because the Supreme Court had the backing of the superior force of the federal government.

But there was more involved than the judgment of the Supreme Court versus that of the state governments. The Court was also displaying some of that "boundless sympathy for humanity" that so appealed to the intellectuals and liberals generally who gave the Court the political support necessary for it to exercise the arbitrary powers it had illegally seized. "Human needs" is one of those undefinable general terms that Rousseau or any of his disciples from Robespierre to the present would have understood and savored. The term might have been found in almost any editorial of the Washington *Post*, or sermon by Bishop John Wesley Lord, or lecture by Professor Arthur Schlesinger, Jr., or speech by Robert F. Kennedy. The latter would have added a flourish, as he did in a speech at Roanoke, Virginia, in celebration of Law Day, when he said that the Supreme Court under Earl Warren "had acted as the conscience of the nation" and "responded to the ethical imperatives of our people." How Rousseau and Robespierre would have loved that!

None of Warren's public addresses is more revealing of his distorted view of the Constitution than his speech before the New York University School of Law in October, 1968. This was one of those phony public events rigged up by liberal supporters of Warren, ostensibly in celebration of the one hundredth anniversary of the adoption of the Fourteenth Amendment to the Constitution, but actually designed to give Warren an opportunity to justify the Supreme Court's use of the Fourteenth Amendment to bring about revolutionary changes in American society. It is certain that this same law school would never celebrate an anniversary of the Tenth Amendment which supposedly guaranteed the rights of the states against encroachment of the federal government, including the judicial branch of that government.

In the New York University speech, Chief Justice Warren, according to a news dispatch, said that "the Supreme Court always stood ready to advance the rights of Negroes and other minority interests if the executive and legislative branches falter." Warren was quoted directly as saying in the course of the speech that the high court's essential function "is to act as the final arbiter of minority rights." After reading these statements, can one doubt that anarchy had entered into the process of judicial interpretation of the Constitution? Here is pure sentimentalism breaking through the hypocritical lip service paid to the sanctity of the Constitution, sacredness of the Bill of Rights, equal justice under law, and equal rights of the rich and the poor. Although Warren had taken an oath to uphold equally the rights of all, he has said here that the Court's primary purpose is to protect minority rights. He would make the Court a partisan of certain groups, rather than a court sworn to render justice to members of the majority as well as minorities, rich as well as poor, white as well as black, Christian as well as atheist, law-abiding citizen as well as lawbreaker, as the framers of the Constitution intended.

Following the fantastic statement that the primary function of the Supreme Court is to protect minority "rights," Warren added: "By remaining a responsive forum of last resort for Negroes and other minority interests, the court can assure that the spirit of the Fourteenth Amendment will become a tangible reality of American life." But what is the spirit of the Fourteenth Amendment? Here again is one of those mushy terms without any precise meaning. What Warren was really saying was that the Supreme Court would continue to exercise an arbitrary rule over the states in all racial matters under precedents established by the Warren Court in its interpretations of the Fourteenth Amendment. In truth, the spirit of the Fourteenth Amendment can be ascertained only by turning the clock back and reading the debates in the 39th Congress at the time the amendment was approved; and this was something that the Warren Court failed to do. Instead, the Court accepted the deliberately distorted version of the debates presented by the NAACP legal staff in the *Brown* case, decided that the intent of the framers was "inconclusive," and turned to the corrupted social sciences as the basis for a decision.

When Warren stated that the Supreme Court would act

in furtherance of minority interests "if the executive and legislative branches falter," (to quote the news dispatch), he was describing an anarchical course of action completely at variance with the constitutional doctrine of the separation of powers and arrogantly claiming the right to take over the functions of the other two branches if necessary to accomplish certain reforms which the Supreme Court considered desirable. How could the Court do this in view of the constitutional limitations placed on the powers of each of the branches of the federal government? It could do this by stretching the Constitution to whatever extent was necessary, knowing that the other branches were no longer controlled by strong men jealous of their own prerogatives and determined to preserve and protect the Constitution and the rights of the states and the people. Dwight D. Eisenhower, John F. Kennedy, and Lyndon B. Johnson were pale shadows of Thomas Jefferson, Andrew Jackson, and Abraham Lincoln.

Earl Warren used the occasion of the New York University speech as an opportunity to polish up his image as a great humanitarian by calling upon all federal, state, and local agencies, including the courts, to undertake a giant brainwashing operation and "employ their total resources" to free the public mind of "racial hatred and mistrust." Here the chief justice is again setting up the courts as social welfare agencies. It is typical of Warren and his authoritarian liberal supporters that they would want this cleansing of the public mind to be done without delay by governmental machinery and force of law rather than the slower voluntary actions of individuals, civic and religious organizations, and private agencies concerned with racial harmony. It is to be regretted that some member of the Warren audience did not ask him this question: "Could not these racial problems be better settled outside the realm of governmental action?" Earl Warren probably would have answered with an explosive "No!" but Edmund Burke would have given an affirmative answer. "It is better," wrote Burke, "to cherish virtue and humanity by leaving much to free will, even with some loss to the object, than to attempt to make men mere machines and instruments of a political benevolence."

Edmund Burke was a much wiser man than Earl Warren and will be long acclaimed as perhaps the greatest political philosopher of this age. Earl Warren will be remembered, if at all, as an unfaithful servant.

In another of his public speeches, Warren stated his belief in that false liberal assumption that property rights and human rights are in conflict. In doing so, he made a sweeping, supercilious condemnation of his predecessors while claiming virtue for himself and his colleagues. "The Supreme Court," he said, "after a tradition of protecting property rights, has become a defender of human rights." Had he bothered to learn more of modern communism, he would have known that human rights do not exist apart from property rights. Once the right to own and use private property is gone—and all property has become the captive of the state—human rights are no more and the right to life itself has disappeared.

Warren's speeches during his chief justiceship reveal an ideological rather than practical view of human nature and the realities of political action. He had been a very successful politician as a district attorney and as attorney general and governor of California. Somewhere along the way he lost his grip, probably because he had permitted himself to become the captive of the doctrinaire intellectuals. His proposal, for example, to employ the total resources of government to rid the public mind of racial distrust is the sheerest liberal utopian nonsense. If all of our governmental resources are to be employed to drive certain mental attitudes and emotions out of the minds of men, must we overlook all of the great problems of state which the federal and state governments were designed to solve? Apparently that is what he thinks, although we cannot be too sure of what he really meant because his New York University speech was primarily an appeal to the liberal "humanitarians" for political support.

In his proposal for brainwashing the public on racial matters, Warren reflected the views of the brotherhood cult, but even this sham creed does not go quite so far because it proposes to use persuasion rather than the powers of government to thrust tolerance into the hearts of the people. When Warren's own arm of the government, the judiciary, attempted to impose a utopian political solution on the racial problem, it brought chaos in our public schools, long-term defiance on the part of a large segment of our population, and a loss of faith in the integrity and good sense of the federal courts and the soundness of our constitutional system.

To quote Edmund Burke once more, this great conservative philosopher observed in his *Reflections on the Revolution in France* that "very plausible schemes, with very pleasing commencements, have often shameful and lamentable conclusions." The French revolutionists, it will be recalled, attempted to impose utopian solutions on the problems of constitutional rule in France, bringing on the Jacobin Reign of Terror, followed by nearly two decades of Bonapartism and nearly two centuries of unstable, often chaotic government.

Will the United States be more successful in overcoming the effects of the judicial lawlessness of the Warren Court than the French have been in surmounting the anarchy introduced into the political life of France by the revolutionary Jacobins? We can hope that one day the American people will perceive the threat of the federal judiciary to their liberties and rid our national life of the petty tyrants and power brokers posing as judges and dispensers of justice under law. Sitting in their magnificent marble temple on Capitol Hill in Washington, the members of the Supreme Court have come to conceive of themselves as little gods beyond the reach of human control. They need to be brought down to earth to live as other mortals. There is surely a serious flaw in a constitutional system that would make it possible for a group of little men such as Earl Warren and his colleagues to wield the tremendous power they held for a decade and a half.

On the Oliver Goldsmith monument in Westminster Abbey there is a Latin epitaph composed by Dr. Samuel Johnson which reads in translation: "He touched nothing that he did not adorn." In contrast, it might be said of Earl Warren and his fellow liberals on the Warren Court, insofar as the performance of their public duties was concerned: "They demeaned everything they touched."

14

Heritage of the New Deal

> A judge's offical conduct should be free from impropriety and the appearance of impropriety. . . .
> Canon 4, Canons of Judicial Ethics
> of the American Bar Association

SINCE JOHN MARSHALL'S DAY the federal judiciary has often allowed political considerations to color its decisions, but it was not until the appearance of the New Deal of Franklin D. Roosevelt that the Supreme Court radically altered its constitutional role by assuming a primary mission of political and social reform. Transformation of the Court from a judicial agency as provided for in the Constitution into a political power center claiming constitution-making, legislative, and executive powers was not sudden but extended over a period of several decades. Beginning as a small stream at the start of Roosevelt's second term in 1937, it reached flood stage with the *Brown* decision of 1954, and at the end of the Warren period had become a raging torrent threatening to destroy those constitutional principles that Americans had long believed would protect their liberties forever. Even the most conservative of the justices on the Warren Court accepted the doctrine that the Court rightfully has a role as a maker of public policy in addition to its prescribed duties as the highest court of law under the Constitution.

Given the radical utopian purposes of the social engineers of the New Deal, and the liberal view that the end justifies the means, it is not surprising that Roosevelt and his advisors would attempt to convert the Court into an instrument of political and social reform. During Roosevelt's first term, the Court, dominated by conservatives, had held a number of New Deal laws unconstitutional. Enraged by what he called the "horse-and-buggy" philosophy of the Court, Roosevelt was determined to bring it under his control. His overwhelming electoral victory in 1936 gave him the confidence to strike hard. In February, 1937, soon after the new Congress met, the president proposed a Court-packing scheme that would increase from nine to fifteen the number of justices on the Court. Six additional justices of the liberal faith would give him the control he desired. However, Congress and the public at large reacted strongly against this proposed change in the makeup of the Court, and Roosevelt was forced to back down for the time being.

While thwarted in his frontal assault on the Court, Roosevelt realized his ambition, nevertheless, for in the next four years seven of the nine justices sitting in 1937 had died or retired. From 1937 to 1941, Roosevelt appointed as associate justices Hugo L. Black of Alabama, Felix Frankfurter of Massachusetts, Stanley Reed of Kentucky, William O. Douglas of Connecticut, Frank Murphy of Michigan, Robert H. Jackson of New York, and James F. Byrnes of South Carolina. Byrnes, the only one of the group who would qualify as a conservative, served only a short time. He resigned in 1942 to become Roosevelt's chief assistant in the war administration and was succeeded by Wiley B. Rutledge of Iowa, one of the more fervent activists. Roosevelt had truly packed the Court with men of his own liberal views, thus assuring the extension of his influence far beyond his own lifetime. When the *Brown* decision was handed down in 1954, five of the justices then on the Court—Black, Frankfurter, Reed, Douglas, and Jackson—were Roosevelt appointees; and two of them, Black and Douglas, were still there as the decade of the 1970s began.

Roosevelt's first Supreme Court appointee was Senator Hugo L. Black of Alabama, one of the more radical of the Senate New Dealers. As a candidate for office in his younger days, Black had joined the then politically powerful Ku Klux Klan, and this fact was brought out during the confirmation hearings in the Senate. This, and the charge that he had had little judicial experience and would be grossly incompetent on the Court, were deeply disturbing to Black who, after he took his seat, was determined to prove his credentials both as a liberal and as a judge. For the next three decades, Black could nearly always be found voting with the radical wing of the Court.

To improve his image among the liberals, Justice Black very early took a public interest in certain far left political activities. Some of Black's relatives were active in the Southern Conference for Human Welfare, a group of leftists which the House Un-American Activities Committee had found to be a Communist-front organization and, in fact, a major recruiting front for Communist party members among Negroes in the South. In March, 1945, according to a news item in the Washington *Afro-American,* the Southern Conference for Human Welfare honored Justice Black with a public banquet and presented him its Jefferson Award for his role in the "civil rights" struggle. At this time and for years to come, Black would be required as a member of the Supreme Court to pass upon numerous cases involving the claims of Negro "civil rights" litigants. In accepting the Jefferson Award from a Communist-oriented, racially biased pressure group, he had publicly compromised his integrity as a justice of our highest court. If he had any qualms of conscience, he never showed them publicly and seemed to take a satanic delight in thumbing his nose at his old friends in Alabama and the South—much in the tradition of Parson Brownlow of the Reconstruction period in Tennessee and Lyndon B. Johnson of more recent days, to name only two of an obnoxious breed. In the Reconstruction period, Black would have been known as a scalawag, a word southerners used to identify traitors and turncoats. It is not an elegant word, but expressive, nevertheless.

Black continued to sit on the Court at a very advanced age, occasionally veering from the dogmatic liberalism of his early days, but still counted among the left-wingers and as a hardliner on the subject of school integration. He did not hesitate to degrade his judicial role by announcing his vote before hearing the evidence. In a 1969 outburst, he angrily announced his intention to support all future Supreme Court decisions that would tend to bring about immediately maximum race mixing in the public schools.

Justice Black resigned from the Court in ill health in September, 1971, and died little more than a week later. He was eighty-five years of age and had been on the Court for thirty-four years. His death and funeral were reported by the liberal media with the usual banality. The news accounts, including the Associated Press dispatches, pictured the former justice as a great strict constructionist, the "peppery champion of individual rights," one who was devoted to "the preservation of the rule of law through the Constitution," who always kept handy his "thumb-worn" copy of the Constitution. One liberal newspaper, published in the Deep South but managed out of New York, proclaimed that he was "truly a giant and will rank among the greatest men ever to sit on the court." Black's career this side of the grave ended on a rather tasteless note. Someone arranged to have pamphlet copies of the Constitution passed out at the funeral home where his body lay in repose. Even at his wake his supporters chose to mar the solemnity of the occasion in an apparent effort to prove his loyalty to the Constitution. As Justice Black's remains were lowered into the grave at Arlington, the Reverend Duncan Howlett, pastor of All Souls' Unitarian Church in Washington, solemnly intoned: "He is no longer ours, now he belongs to eternity."

Roosevelt's second appointment to the Supreme Court "made the conservatives of that day tremble," as a liberal reporter for the Washington *Post* phrased it. This appointment was none other than Felix Frankfurter, controversial professor of law at Harvard, "civil rights" agitator, political busybody, and Franklin D. Roosevelt's errand boy and speechwriter. Frankfurter was a vain and arrogant man, but he had much to be vain about. An immigrant from Austria, he had risen to the top of his profession when he became professor of law at Harvard at a time when this oldest American university was still considered to be the very citadel of the New England spirit. In the Sacco-Vanzetti controversy, Frankfurter and his fellow radicals had scored a great political victory over the old New England establishment that probably destroyed its power forever. Today, when the heirs of the Yankee tradition such as the Lodges, Peabodys, and Binghams seek public office, they must bow down before the newer immigrant groups, kowtow to the black voters, and pay respects to the latest twist in the liberal line. Even then, the New England electorate is more likely to turn to the most liberal candidate on the list, regardless of race, religion, or political party. The New England soul has been fragmented, and a grave moral and political permissiveness now extends over much of the region once dominated by those stern children of God, the Puritans. It is not surprising that New England's most popular political figure in recent years has been Senator Edward M. Kennedy of Massachusetts.

Felix Frankfurter had many of the character traits of his chief, Earl Warren. Both were pompous and humorless men, highly susceptible to flattery; and both lacked that inner grace that manifests itself outwardly in humility, constraint, and the ancient Greek virtue of piety. Neither had the Greek tragic or comic sense of life. Felix Frankfurter's life in America can be understood only as melodrama—the brash, ambitious, and pushing underdog who became the posturing, opinionated top dog by means of a sharp intelligence, energy, cunning, and outright gall.

Frankfurter selected Max Freedman, a party-line liberal journalist, as his biographer and the editor of his papers. Freedman, in his writings, speeches, and editorial annotations of the Frankfurter letters, attempted to turn his hero into a little tin god; but in the published Roosevelt-Frankfurter correspondence he revealed one incident that showed Frankfurter in a very bad light, as wanting in intellectual and moral integrity. When Roosevelt's 1937 Court-packing plan was submitted to Congress, Frankfurter assumed a public pose of neutrality and insisted until the day of his death that he had been neutral in this cynical attempt of the executive branch to destroy the independence of the judiciary and to bring the Supreme Court under presidential control. But in fact he was dissembling, as revealed in the published correspondence. When Roosevelt, with characteristic cynicism, asked Frankfurter to prepare a written defense of the plan, the latter complied, believing that his double role of being simultaneously neutral and a defender of Roosevelt's attack on the Court would not be publicly revealed at the time, and perhaps never. Freedman attempted to exonerate Frankfurter, but had to admit that "there is a good deal wrong . . . with being a secret partisan while wearing the disguise of public neutrality. . . ."

Frankfurter had been one of the founders of the American Civil Liberties Union, a policy adviser of the NAACP for many years, and had had a leading role in the whole of the modern "civil rights" movement that came to life after the First World War. Yet, after he was appointed to the Court, he followed Justice Black's lead and at no time seriously considered disqualifying himself in "civil rights" cases. It was his pretense, no doubt, that once he donned the black robes, he put aside his lifelong beliefs and assumed the role of the completely detached judge. One of the current liberal legends is that Frankfurter, on the bench, became a strong conservative and a believer in judicial restraint. It is true, in his later years on the Court, Frankfurter became somewhat alarmed at the growing public criticism of the controversial decrees that came pouring from the judicial hopper. In a number of cases, such as those involving legislative apportionment, he sided with the more conservative wing, and he even became known for a time as the principal opponent of Chief Justice Earl Warren's devil-may-care activism. Nevertheless, during his long tenure on the Court, which lasted from 1939 to his retirement in 1962, Felix Frankfurter usually lined up with the liberals and was one of the New Dealers who turned the Court into a social welfare agency.

Of all the Roosevelt men on the Supreme Court, there is no doubt that William O. Douglas was the most consistently radical, always voting with the extreme left and sometimes handing down dissenting opinions that made his fellow liberals appear as ultra-conservatives. Douglas was not satisfied with banning prayer and Bible-reading in the public schools; he would have gone all the way to insure the death of God in public affairs by eliminating all references to the Deity on the coinage, at all public functions, and in the armed services.

Douglas was a professor of law at Yale University when Roosevelt brought him into the New Deal as chairman of the Securities Exchange Commission from whence he was elevated to the Supreme Court. While consistent in his radicalism on the bench, in his personal life he has been quite erratic. His flawed character is basically cynical, frivolous, and at times venal. His quest for money—based in part on his liability for alimony payments to three former wives—has led him into many acts that compromised his integrity as a judge and as a man, but he has gone his merry way and if he has had any regrets they have not been revealed to the public.

Douglas has appeared wholly unaware of the extreme impropriety of a justice of the Supreme Court accepting monetary awards and testimonial dinners from organizations involved in litigation or otherwise vitally interested in court cases that would eventually come before the high Court. Fairly early in his career as a Supreme Court justice, Douglas became virtually a protege of the Congress of Industrial Organizations (CIO). At the 1948 national convention of the CIO at Portland, Oregon, Douglas was the guest of honor and gave the principal address. His strongly partisan speech brought down the house. Two years later, the CIO presented Douglas with the $1,000 Sidney Hillman Award for "meritorious public service." At this time, the CIO had a strong interest in the litigation involving school segregation and gave monetary support to the NAACP Legal Defense Fund, including a gift of $75,000 contributed through the CIO's Murray Foundation, a tax-free organization. One may presume that any Supreme Court decision involving the CIO's interests and in which Douglas participated would be tainted justice.

In 1961 Justice Douglas accepted the presidency of the Nevada-based Parvin Foundation whose principal and perhaps sole income was from stockholdings in a firm owning three gambling casinos in Las Vegas. The Parvin Foundation had acquired these holdings through the agency of a well-known gangster, Meyer Lansky. Douglas was the only paid official of the foundation and received a salary of $12,000 or more a year. Over a period of seven years he was paid a total salary of $85,000. There is reason to believe that Douglas was only a figurehead and that the foundation was run by its founder, Albert Parvin, who served as its vice president. In short, Douglas was lending his prestige as a justice of the Supreme Court for a very large fee.

The Parvin Foundation had close ties with and was a contributor to the Center for the Study of Democratic Institutions, a tax-free, left-wing group that also poured money into Douglas' pockets. For example, in two four-day seminars held early in 1969, Douglas received consultant fees of $500 per day, which amounted to a total of $4,000, plus $865 for travel expenses. Douglas had been made the figurehead chairman of the board of both the center, based at Santa Barbara, California, and the Fund for the Republic, the parent organization of the center.

In May, 1969, at the time of the Justice Abe Fortas scandal, the press began to dig out and publish the facts about Douglas' relations with the Parvin Foundation and the Center for the Study of Democratic Institutions. He was forced by public pressure to resign from both organizations, but he refused to follow Fortas' lead and resign from the Supreme Court. One wag suggested that the forced reduction in Douglas' income would have amounted to cruel and unusual punishment because he needed the money for alimony payments to his former wives.

Another questionable practice of Justice Douglas was his frequent, intemperate attacks on United States foreign policy and many aspects of domestic policy. Although he usually had no competence or expertise in the areas in which he expounded his views, he never hesitated to express his opinions in the most extravagant language. His political statements, speeches, and writings have been always on the extreme left and have been designed to appeal to radical groups. In 1969 or perhaps earlier, he began to take an active interest in stirring up and encouraging the student revolution. In a speech at Case Western Reserve University Law School, he told the radical student leaders that they alone had the spirit and competence to bring about the revolutionary changes needed in the present university curriculum. In another speech, at the University of Maine, in which he blasted the students' "politically bankrupt elders," he attacked the foreign and military policies of both Johnson and Nixon, the Vietnam War, the selective service system, and the military-industrial complex. And what was his own solution to our present problems, as revealed in his University of Maine speech? A brace of utopian socialistic cliches that might have been put forward by the blindest advocate of the United Nations. He would have us "go to work on cooperative projects" and "search for common grounds through rules of law that bind all mankind together and take the place of war." Not even U Thant would have perpetrated that.

In his book *Points of Rebellion* (1970), Douglas declared himself to be a strong believer in revolution as possibly the only remaining means of bringing about needed changes in the American political and social order. He thus, toward the end of his long career on the bench, rejected the law he had sworn to uphold but which he steadily subverted over the years. In truth, his book—actually a 97-page booklet outrageously priced at $4.95—was no more than a rehash of recent political speeches and writings and was no doubt designed to catch the market made up of turbulent radicals on the campuses looking for justification for their barbaric acts. If the justification is supplied by a justice of the United States Supreme Court, so much the better.

Two other Roosevelt appointees on the Supreme Court at the time of the *Brown* decision were Stanley F. Reed of Kentucky and Robert H. Jackson of New York. Both had been solicitors general in the Roosevelt administration and Jackson had been attorney general. Both were less flamboyant individuals than their colleagues Black, Frankfurter, and Douglas. Neither had been a member of the Ku Klux Klan, had built a national reputation as a flaming radical agitator in the "civil rights" field, nor had Douglas' reputation as an associate and beneficiary of unsavory financial and political figures. Nevertheless, both were faithful liberal followers of Franklin D. Roosevelt in the Justice Department and on the Supreme Court. Justice Jackson yielded to none in his belief in the social reform mission of the judiciary, and he was possibly as innovative as any of the New Deal justices in developing an intellectual underpinning for the activist philosophy.

15

Abe Fortas Scandal

> Small wonder that the Supreme Court of the United States has steadily fallen into disrepute in recent years as it has developed into an oligarchy of politically rather than judicially minded individuals. Now President Johnson has selected Abe Fortas—his personal friend of long standing who has never had a day's experience on the bench—to be one of the nine justices of the Supreme Court of the United States. This is in line with the unfortunate turns of the past several years.
>
> David Lawrence (1965)

ABE FORTAS WAS THE MOST CONTROVERSIAL FIGURE to sit on the United States Supreme Court since Jefferson's term as president and the first in history to be forced to resign under public pressure. He came into the government under the New Deal, although it was not until some years later that he was appointed to the Supreme Court by President Lyndon B. Johnson. He possessed a sharp mind but a rather flexible set of principles and a rubbery character. After graduation from Yale Law School, where he studied under William O. Douglas, Fortas became one of the young radicals in the legal division of the Agricultural Adjustment Administration in the earliest days of the New Deal. This group included Alger Hiss, Lee Pressman, John Abt, and Nathan Witt, all of whom were later identified as Communists. Fortas himself was a member of a number of Communist-front organizations.

Fortas later served as under secretary of the Department of the Interior in the New Deal, but his real rise to power began with his association with Lyndon B. Johnson, whom he served as attorney and fixer. After Johnson was elected to the Senate in 1948—in a highly controversial election decision in which Fortas acted as Johnson's attorney—Johnson rose fast in the political jungles of Washington as Senate majority leader, vice president, and president; and Fortas rose with him. Fortas performed many tasks for Johnson over the years, but probably the one most revealing of the character of both Johnson and Fortas, as well as their friend Drew Pearson, was the destruction of Don Reynolds, an insurance agent who had sold Johnson a very large life insurance policy with a premium kickback arrangement. Reynolds had consented to testify in the 1964 hearings on Bobby Baker, former Senate majority clerk and friend of Johnson, and there was some fear that the testimony might reveal some damaging information on President Johnson. Whereupon, the Johnson organization, which included Bobby Baker's attorney Abe Fortas, obtained certain information from Reynolds' army personnel file that reflected on Reynolds' character and military career. This material found its way to Drew Pearson who published it in his column, and Reynolds was so cowed that he disappeared from public view. This was an incident right out of *Advise and Consent,* the Allen Drury novel which contained in its plot a portrayal of presidential blackmail. All involved in the Reynolds case were in clear violation of the law, because military personnel files are marked CONFIDENTIAL and are not releasable to the public except under certain strict conditions which were not met here.

Abe Fortas was well acquainted with the editors of Washington newspapers and used his acquaintanceships at least twice in attempts to cover up scandals in which Lyndon B. Johnson was involved. He was unsuccessful in both of these attempts, but he may have been successful in other instances which did not become public knowledge. After Don Reynolds had sold Lyndon B. Johnson the life insurance policy, Bobby Baker persuaded Reynolds to present to the Johnson family an expensive stereo set. When news of this "gift" to Lyndon and Lady Bird reached the papers, Fortas tried to suppress the story but was unsuccessful.

In the fall of 1964, during the presidential campaign, Fortas again tried to put a "fix" on the Washington daily papers to prevent publication of the news of the second arrest of presidential aide Walter Jenkins for homosexuality. Fortas had the assistance of Clark Clifford, a highly successful Washington influence peddler whom Johnson later appointed secretary of defense, but the newspapers refused to suppress the story.

When Arthur Goldberg resigned as associate justice of the Supreme Court in 1965 to become United States ambassador to the United Nations, President Johnson appointed Abe Fortas to succeed him. Rumors had been floating around that Fortas would get the appointment, but those who were familiar with Fortas' career could not believe that Johnson would have the impudence to appoint to a position of such power and prestige a crony and an influence-peddler. But that was because many people did not fully realize that President Johnson was a man not unlike Abe Fortas, with an equal amount of gall, whose first principle was to take care of himself, family, and friends at public expense. Fortas was appointed and confirmed by the Senate. As expected, he voted almost 100 percent with Earl Warren and the doctrinaire liberals on the Court.

Johnson's boldness grew with his success in getting Abe Fortas onto the Supreme Court as an associate justice. Several years later, in June, 1968, when Earl Warren announced his intention to retire as soon as his successor was confirmed,

Johnson nominated Fortas to succeed Warren as chief justice, to the dismay and anger of millions of Americans. It was sheer effrontery, and Johnson soon knew that he had made a serious mistake. The Senate Judiciary Committee revealed that Fortas, while on the Court, had continued to act as Johnson's fixer and intermediary in clear violation of the doctrine of the separation of powers. It soon came out, too, that one of Fortas' former law partners, Paul Porter, had raised a sum of $15,000 from Fortas' wealthy friends to finance a series of lectures by Fortas at American University in Washington, D.C. This was obviously a payoff to Fortas for favors rendered and to be rendered, and much of the cost would fall on the taxpayers because the contributions to American University were tax deductible. Johnson was forced by public pressure to withdraw the Fortas nomination, and Chief Justice Earl Warren stayed on until June, 1969, at which time President Nixon appointed Warren E. Burger to succeed him.

Every public move involving Fortas at this time, even the resignation of Chief Justice Earl Warren, seemed to be touched with scandal. Warren's resignation was not direct and forthright, but was to become effective only upon the confirmation of his successor by the Senate. This appeared to many to be a threat by the chief justice to carry out his announced intention to resign only if his successor were a man of the liberal left who would continue the Warren activist course. Whatever his intentions, Warren was in actuality in a position to veto any appointment not meeting his approval. When President Johnson announced the nomination of Fortas as Warren's successor, conservatives accused the triumvirate—Johnson, Warren, and Fortas—of a conspiracy to force the Senate to approve Fortas or endure the continuance of Warren as chief justice for an indefinite period. Fortunately, all three men were forced by public opinion to abandon this apparent attempt to violate the spirit if not the letter of the Constitution.

His failure to achieve the chief justiceship was undoubtedly a bitter disappointment to Abe Fortas, but his troubles had only begun with this setback to his lofty ambitions. Early in May, 1969, *Life* magazine revealed that within three months after Fortas had become an associate justice, he had accepted a check for $20,000 from the Wolfson Family Foundation, a tax-free charitable agency (at least, chartered as such) set up by Louis Wolfson, a high-flying financier, and his brothers. Ostensibly, Fortas had been hired as a consultant to the foundation to give advice on charitable and educational activities in which he claimed to be interested. After the *Life* expose, Paul Porter identified one of the Fortas interests as a program for granting scholarships for theological studies, and Mrs. Fortas quickly added that her husband's role was also one of advising the trustees on possible "civil rights" projects.

The truth is, at the time Fortas was hired by the foundation, Louis Wolfson was under investigation by the Securities Exchange Commission for possible violation of federal securities laws. Some months after the payment to Fortas, Wolfson told one his associates, who had inquired about the SEC investigation, that the matter was going to be taken care of "at the top" and would never get out of Washington. Nevertheless, in the fall of 1966 Wolfson and several of his associates were indicted on criminal charges, and in December of that year Fortas returned the $20,000, eleven months after receiving it. After the publication of the *Life* article, Fortas, in an effort to brazen through, publicly stated that he had only been "tendered a fee" by Wolfson, and that he had rejected it because he was too busy to perform the duties of consultant. But under public pressure he finally broke down and admitted that he was to be paid $20,000 a year for life, and that the payments were to continue to his wife after his death if she survived him. He resigned in disgrace and left the public scene, probably forever, although one can never be certain when and under what circumstances a man of his tastes for intrigue, money, and power will turn up again.

16

Educationists and the Schools

> I do not feel the so-called establishment has to be dismantled, but I do feel that we must change it dramatically. In my new position as spokesman for education at the national level, I intend to be an active and vocal advocate for such a change....
>
> If busing is the best way to eliminate segregation, to provide better education in an integrated setting, then it should be employed to whatever extent is necessary.
>
> Dr. James E. Allen, Jr., United States Commissioner of Education, 1969–1970, by appointment of President Richard M. Nixon

AMONG THE MORE ARDENT SUPPORTERS of federal court interference in the public schools and their consequent disruption have been the leaders of the educational bureaucracy in Washington—comprised of the National Education Association, a politically powerful but nevertheless tax-free lobby, and its operating arm within the government, the Office of Education. This double-headed monster has not been ruled in recent years by well-educated scholars, but by educationist empire builders and sociological-minded administrators who are incapable of communicating with the clarity of the true scholar but who employ in the spoken and written word what columnist James J. Kilpatrick has called "educationist Swahili that passes for professional English." The most profound thought that has come out of this bureaucratic jungle was expressed by Dr. James E. Allen, Jr., President Nixon's first commissioner of education, who insisted that we must have the "awareness of the need for change" of the young generation in order to "revitalize our society and gain more quickly the improvements that are so desperately needed." He didn't specify the changes needed, but we may surmise that any change would be desirable as long as it projected us farther into the utopian dream world of the liberal imagination.

The last educator to fill the office of commissioner of education resigned in September, 1962, rather than permit his office to be run by a small group of executives of the National Education Association who wanted power without responsibility. He was succeeded by a trio of the most dedicated bureaucrats and social experimenters in the history of the office of education and of the federal government as a whole. These were: Francis Keppel, appointed by Kennedy in 1963 and fired by Johnson in 1965 for political ineptitude; Harold Howe II, the most extreme of them all, who served the Johnson administration from 1965 to 1969; and Dr. James E. Allen, Jr., appointed by Nixon at the beginning of his term in 1969 and fired by the administration in June, 1970, for publicly criticizing the president in the Cambodian operation, a subject wholly outside the area of Dr. Allen's authority and competence.

Francis Keppel's primary interest was "civil rights" rather than education, and he will probably be best remembered, if at all, for his "Thank God for the civil rights movement" exclamation before the annual meeting of the American Association of School Administrators in 1964. The educational philosophy of Keppel was revealed in a typical speech at a 1964 meeting promoted by the NAACP to mark the tenth anniversary of the *Brown* decision. Keppel proposed a "working partnership between education and the civil rights movement," thus advancing the political concept that the public schools should become agencies for social reform rather than education. He was, in fact, doing no more than propounding the philosophy of his fellow liberals of the Warren Court. In this speech, Keppel laid out a six-point program to make education "a creative agent for change." He advanced a dramatic "new design" for public education in which he was actually borrowing ideas from the "Higher Horizons" program of the New York City schools, a program that turned out to be a complete failure and was abandoned. Keppel touched all the bases of the liberal activists. He admitted that education had been hesitant and immobilized in the face of "overwhelming evidence of the need for change," without citing the evidence. He viewed school boycotts of black students, parents' marches, and teacher strikes as no more than "creative tensions," another liberal favorite; but, of course, protests must not be allowed to "degenerate into destructive hostility." Above all, we must "shape new dimensions for all our children."

Harold Howe II, son of a white president of a Negro college, had grown up in the belief in the divinity of race mixing. He had been involved in various integration experiments prior to his appointment as commissioner of education. He would now have the opportunity to carry out his experiments on a grand scale, especially after the Warren Court decision in the *Green* and related cases in 1968 requiring the states to take positive steps to bring about maximum integration. Whereas in *Brown* the Court had said that race may not be used as a criterion for school assignment, in *Green* the Court reversed itself and said that race must be the criterion for assignment in those states where *de jure* segregation had existed. Howe welcomed the decision and employed every power at his command, embodied in his "guidelines" to bring about the maximum mixing of the races in the schools. He was ruthless and unmerciful in applying the office of education dictates, which he and his staff made as uncompromising as possible.

In the 1968 presidential campaign, Richard M. Nixon appeared to promise some relief to the schools by curbing the federal bureaucrats, but this was only campaign oratory. After he was elected, Nixon appointed Robert H. Finch, a liberal Republican politician, as his secretary of the Department of Health, Education and Welfare; and none other than "Mr. Busing" himself, Dr. James E. Allen, Jr., as commissioner of education. From the viewpoints of the harassed school officials and worried parents, it would be hard to imagine two worse appointments. Dr. Allen, son of the president of a small college in West Virginia, had been for some years New York state commissioner of education in the Rockefeller administration. As such, he had taken an active role in forcing the maximum mixing of the races in state schools. In 1963 he sent a memorandum to all state school officials requiring them to take active steps to bring about racial balance in the schools. He declared that racial imbalance existed when any school had 50 percent or more Negro pupils. He was an ardent advocate of busing as a means of reducing racial imbalance and so earned his nickname of "Mr. Busing."

Dr. Allen's prose was saturated with the same educationist jargon found in that of his two immediate predecessors and, for that matter, all of the liberal school bureaucrats. He was all for the "new breed" of students, meaning he preferred the foul-mouthed campus mobsters to the serious, law-abiding students. He liked not only their "awareness of the need for change," quoted above, but their desire to participate in "achieving humanistic solutions" for the problems of school and society. These non-thoughts could as easily have come from the minds of Francis Keppel and Harold Howe. What Dr. Allen was really trying to say was that he and his fellow innovators of the left welcomed the support of the student anarchists in their efforts to gain complete control of the schools so that they, the educational bureaucrats, would be free to carry out their radical experiments in social engineering regardless of the cost to students, parents, and taxpayers.

If the educational leaders of the country have no desire to preserve our schools as educational institutions, who is left to save them? Certainly not the political leaders in Congress and the executive branch in recent years, most of whom have supported the Supreme Court's racial decisions in their mad play for the black vote. One of the major scandals of this period of American history has been the willingness of the liberal leaders in Congress to turn the children of the country over to the tender mercies of the federal Courts and the HEW bureaucrats for sociological experiments in race mixing, while sending their own children to virtually all-white private schools, thus avoiding the dangers of the racial cockpits which the public schools have become in the Washington area. Among the liberal politicians who send their children to private or suburban schools to avoid the integration they demand of others are such leading Democrats as Senator Edmund Muskie, former Senator Eugene McCarthy, Senator Birch Bayh, Senator Edward Kennedy and 1972 Presidential nominee George McGovern.

Although the hypocrisy of individual liberal leaders on school integration has been made public from time to time, the extent of it in our capital city was revealed for the first time by Mike Wallace, CBS television reporter, in a 1971 broadcast (even here Mr. Wallace exposed only the tip of the iceberg). Other liberal leaders found to be as guilty as members of Congress included federal judges, civic leaders, and journalists, black as well as white. The editor, an editorial writer, and a columnist of the Washington *Post*—the most ardent journalistic advocate of school integration over the years—refused to send their own children to school with black children. When asked why, the *Post* columnist replied frankly: "Nobody wants to make their children pay for their own social philosophy." Among the black liberals found to be sending their own children to predominantly white private schools were Associate Justice Thurgood Marshall of the United States Supreme Court, Mayor Walter Washington of the city of Washington, Congressman Walter Fauntroy who represents the District of Columbia, and Carl Rowan, leading Negro newspaper columnist.

To return to the subject of the future of our public schools, they will not be saved by the wealthy and powerful upper-class leaders of the liberal establishment—the Rockefellers, Harrimans, Kennedys, Fords, Dillons, and the press and television barons—and their fellow activists of the middle class scattered through the federal and state bureaucracies, foundations, universities, churches, publishing houses, and communications media. These look upon the schools as objects of manipulation to bring about and preserve conditions favorable to the continued rule of the present liberal power structure that dominates both major parties. Such conditions include a contented black minority, spoon-fed with integration and other social uplift schemes, plus a torpid white majority from the politically passive middle and working classes.

If the public schools are saved (and there is an increasing number who believe that these schools are not worth saving in their present form) it will come as the result of the efforts of the concerned parents of the country, white and black, middle class and working class. Parents will have to work with responsible citizens at the community level who are able to observe at first hand the racial turmoil and disorder in the classrooms—the failure to educate, the harassed school officials, the unhappy teachers, the confused pupils, the despairing parents, the newest school buildings standing vacant while children are bused to distant schools in order to achieve maximum race mixing, white history and traditions crammed into the minds of black students in some schools, and black studies forced upon white students in others.

These conditions must be blamed in large part on the federal courts, which took the lead in turning the schools over to the social experimenters whose manipulations have taken precedent over the cause of education. Instead of checking the unconstitutional encroachments of the federal judiciary, the executive and legislative branches have joined in the sport under pressure from the intellectuals, the black leaders, the labor union hierarchy, and "civil rights" advocates generally. What the judicial and other meddlers have actually done is to create a condition in which both public education and civil rights in the true sense are going down the drain. The trend will be reversed when the majority of the people become fully conscious of the present anarchy that threatens our constitutional system, especially the judicial debasement of our state governments within that system, and elects men to public office who will be guided by wisdom, experience, tradition, and common sense, rather than the so-called "humanistic solutions" of the liberal ideologues, educationists, social scientists, and social experimenters generally.

17

Loss of Faith in the Federal Courts

> ... if the policy of the government . . . is to be irrevocably fixed by decisions of the Supreme Court . . . the people will have ceased to be their own rulers, having to that extent practically resigned their government into the hands of that eminent tribunal.
>
> Abraham Lincoln, First Inaugural Address (1861)

ONE OF THE UNFORTUNATE CONSEQUENCES of the rulings of the Warren Court has been the loss of faith of so many Americans in the discretion and ordinary common sense of our federal judges. This includes the judges in the lower courts, many of whom have been more arrogant and capricious in their rulings than the activists on the Supreme Court. Loss of faith in our federal judiciary may not be as obvious as some of the other evils that have followed from the Warren rule, but it may prove more damaging in the long run.

In the present crisis, there has been a steady erosion of the faith of the people in a government of limited powers under a fixed Constitution which our founding fathers thought, or at least hoped, would guarantee our liberties for ages to come. The concept that the widest possible diffusion of power would form a permanent bar to tyranny has been largely shattered by the federal courts. Suddenly, after a decade and a half of gradual encroachment, the American people found in 1954 that a government by judicial rule, so much feared by Thomas Jefferson, had been thrust upon them. Legislative and executive powers were seized by the courts at the expense of the other branches; and the states, which had brought the Constitution into being, found their reserved powers reduced to nothingness in those areas in which the federal judges elected to assert their authority.

The Constitution had assigned the judicial branch a role apart from the power struggles of the political elements—the elected legislative and executive branches and the state governments. But driven on by the liberal intellectuals and other minority groups, the Warren Court set itself up as a center of political power in direct competition with the political branches and the states. In an article in the *Virginia Law Review* in 1954, Professor Carl Brent Swisher, constitutional historian, derided the Court for its "bizarre behavior" in its reach for power and concluded: "It stands exposed as a power group competing with other groups wielding political power in our society."

The Warren Court's political support came almost wholly from the left, and as long as the political power of the left continued to rise, that of the Supreme Court rose with it, for neither Congress nor the president had the political muscle or the will to curb it and bring it back within the bounds of the Constitution. In the year 1969, with the appointment of Warren E. Burger to succeed Earl Warren as chief justice, the tide appeared to be turning at last, although one could not be sure, especially after the new chief justice voted with the liberal activists in the Mississippi schools case, the first in which he participated, and wrote the Court's unanimous decision in 1971 approving school busing. Back in 1953, there had been some who thought that Earl Warren would have a restraining influence on the Court. President Nixon's appointment of Burger to succeed Warren, whether it turns the tide or not, seemed at the time to have the approbation of the great majority of the American people precisely because they thought he would be more restrained and would reverse, or at least slow down, the activist trend of the Supreme Court under Warren. At the same time, there appeared to have been a general sense of relief as Warren stepped down.

Accompanying the loss of faith in the integrity of our federal judges has been the development of a sense of contempt where respect had existed before. Millions of Americans now look on the deliberations of our federal courts not as a dispensation of justice but as a farce, the triumph of political partisanship, dishonesty, and nitpicking over ordinary common sense. This change in attitude is illustrated by an earthy comment of columnist Tom Ethridge in the April 1, 1969, issue of the Jackson, Mississippi, *Clarion-Ledger:* "never underestimate the U.S. Supreme Court's capacity for judicial jackassery." The comment was made in connection with a discussion of whether the Warren Court would seriously consider on appeal a suit filed in a lower federal court claiming that police action against a prostitute had violated her civil rights guaranteed by the Constitution.

In a 1969 decision the United States Supreme Court found in the Constitution a rule that a school principal cannot constitutionally suspend students who insist upon wearing armbands bearing anti-Vietnam War slogans on campus in violation of school regulations. The decision was written by the then Associate Justice Abe Fortas and was approved by a seven-to-two majority of the Court. Trivial legal actions such as this have been even more common in the lower federal courts. Federal district Judge Frank M. Johnson, Jr., of Montgomery, Alabama, provides a good example of a meddlesome lower court judge short on humility and ordinary common sense. He and other radical members of the federal judiciary in the South have earned the utter contempt of much of the population.

Judge Johnson has not hesitated to embarrass college presidents, school principals, and local school boards by overturning their administrative decisions in the pettiest, most trivial cases. An Alabama high school principal had suspended a student for refusing to cut his long hair to a length prescribed by school regulations. The boy took the case to federal court and Judge Johnson ordered the principal to reinstate him on the grounds that his constitutional rights had been violated.

Two of Judge Johnson's bizarre decrees denied the authority of college presidents to make normal administrative decisions. At Tuskegee Institute, a Negro school founded by Booker T. Washington, a group of militant troublemakers, angry because some of their impudent demands had been rejected, stormed the administration building while the board of trustees was holding its annual meeting. The students padlocked the building and held captive for thirteen hours the president and eleven other trustees. After this and other violent incidents that followed, the school was closed for two weeks during which a thorough investigation was made and the guilty identified. When classes resumed, fifty-four students were barred. The students took their cases to federal court, and Judge Johnson ordered them reinstated pending the holding of formal hearings and the presentation of evidence that the students were guilty of dismissable conduct. "The law is basic," said Judge Johnson, that students cannot be "deprived of their status and their rights" without hearings. This is pernicious doctrine which implies that formal legal hearings must be employed in all controversies involving teacher and pupil in educational institutions, private as well as public. The most mischievous consequences could flow from such a doctrine should it become the law of the land.

Daniel Webster once said: "The attainment of knowledge does not comprise all which is contained in the large term of education. The feelings are to be disciplined; the passions are to be restrained; true and worthy motives are to be inspired; a profound religious feeling is to be instilled; and pure morality included, under all circumstances. All this is comprised in education." Some such broad concept of education was probably in the mind of President Harry Philpott of Auburn University when, early in 1969, he barred as a speaker on the Auburn campus the Reverend William Sloane Coffin, chaplain of Yale University. Reverend Coffin had recently been convicted of the felony of publicly advocating violation of the selective service law. President Philpott did not want his students or the public to believe that the university was giving its sanction to the radical views of a convicted felon. Furthermore, he feared possible demonstrations and disorderly protests on campus. The American Civil Liberties Union, that disputatious group of busybodies always ready to spring to the defense of leftist radicals, brought suit in Judge Johnson's court to overrule the disbarment of Coffin. Judge Johnson held that President Philpott's administrative action violated the First Amendment and was not regulation of conduct on campus but constituted "blatant political censorship." In this case an eccentric exhibitionist in the black robes of a federal judge was quite willing to base a verdict on a farfetched interpretation of the First Amendment, make it possible for a felon to stir up the passions of a group of rowdy university students, and publicly embarrass the president of a great university in a matter involving a rather trifling administrative decision. Reverend Coffin appeared on campus on schedule and blasted the United States government and our military forces for our part in the Vietnam War.

In a typical doctrinaire liberal news dispatch, the UPI news service reported that Coffin "received a rousing reception from students," without revealing the size of the audience, the extent to which the audience was dominated by campus radicals, or the approximate number of non-student radicals who had come to applaud. Reasonable estimates could (and should) have been made of these factors by a competent reporter. Through this limited reporting, the reader was led to believe that a large number of Auburn students approved of Reverend Coffin and his activities. Although Auburn University has not escaped the student revolution, the great majority of Auburn students are loyal citizens, long known for their strong sense of duty and devotion to country. They are not the emotionally retarded zombies who dominate the campuses of so many of our politicized universities.

A people will forgive almost anything in their rulers if they believe that the rulers are acting with good sense where the permanent, long-range interests of the nation are involved. But the people become alarmed and rapidly lose faith if they think that those in authority are moved not by right reason but by whimsy, not by statecraft but by ideology, not by wisdom but by shallow sophistry, and not by the Constitution and legal precedent but by the corrupted social sciences and shallow sentiments of the judges. A politically alert people will not permanently tolerate a judiciary that bases its most far-reaching decisions, involving public peace and good order in the state, on the fancied interests of vocal, aggressive minority pressure groups, or even temporary majorities. To be specific, the American people have not been happy to see their federal judges become political jumping jacks subject to the manipulations of the NAACP, the American Civil Liberties Union, the Americans for Democratic Action, the Anti-Defamation League, the League of Women Voters, the National Education Association, and the National Council of Churches.

In truth, more often than not the highly vocal and often self-appointed spokesmen for the political interests of racial, religious, or other groups do not represent the true interests of the group but only the fancied interests of the elite leadership. Certainly, the National Council of Churches does not represent the true interests or the dominant ideas of the forty million or more Protestants it claims to represent. The loss of faith of millions of Americans in the good sense of our highest judges has extended also to our church leaders, many of whom have forsworn their duty to God in an attempt to bring about salvation on earth by radical action in the political field.

Given the present turmoil in the schools and the virtual breakdown of the public school system in many areas, can it be said that Thurgood Marshall, Jack Greenberg, and the other NAACP lawyers and their hired academic intellectuals truly represented the interests of the Negro children and their parents in the *Brown* decision? There are many Negro parents who do not think so. The Negro pupils, not the white, have been and will continue to be the principal victims of the public school breakdown because they are nearly wholly dependent on tax-supported public schools for an education, while a large number of the white children have withdrawn or could withdraw to private schools. The black students have been the victims of the hot-eyed liberal ideologues, the federal courts, the left-wing politicians of both parties seeking black votes, a succession of weak presidents, and those members of the black elite who are intent on seizing political power while riding on the backs of the black masses. Many black leaders, including the militants, and their followers have come to realize that integration has brought more problems than it has settled. Many blacks are now moving toward resegregation in an effort to save their pride and self-respect and to build a sense of community that will meet their own educational and emotional needs. Many responsible black parents now see that their children will never develop into self-respecting members of our pluralistic society in integrated schools which, in the North, are dominated by white liberals who are more interested in doctrinaire concepts of race mixing than in education. In the South, the integrated schools in most cases are controlled by a white majority whose history is not black history, whose values do not coincide with black values, and whose aspirations clash with black aspirations.

In the state of Mississippi, after the Supreme Court decision in the Mississippi schools case ordering the establishment of "unitary" schools forthwith, many of the white parents began to shift their children to private schools. At the same time, in at least one Mississippi county and probably others, many of the more affluent black parents, *including the majority of the black teachers in the public schools,* began transferring their children from the public schools to private Catholic schools. This was revealed in a letter from "A Concerned Negro Parent" of Madison County, Mississippi, to the Jackson *Clarion-Ledger* which appeared in the April 16, 1970, issue. Both white and black parents knew, as the letter pointed out, that quality education would be impossible in the heat of racial conflict that would develop in the integrated schools. The purpose of the letter was to plead for white-black cooperation in an effort to save the public schools. All involved knew that they could be saved only under some plan of community control attuned to local conditions. Forced congregation by federal power might be maintained for a period of time, but the schools would no longer be able to educate in the hostile atmosphere that would intensify rather than diminish.

Unfortunately, too many blacks today believe that their long-range interests will best be served by a highly centralized government possessing unlimited coercive powers. Such a government might presently be in the hands of friends but could readily be taken over by enemies. While the political tide has been running in favor of the blacks since the New Deal, they might find suddenly, as the Ku Klux Klan discovered in the 1920s and as the prohibitionists found in the early 1930s, that public opinion can change overnight and that political demands that are taken seriously today might be treated with contempt tomorrow.

It is doubtful that the United States Supreme Court has ever been held in such low esteem as at the present time, although on other occasions its prestige had suffered greatly when it attempted to interfere in political controversies in which great issues were involved and which were, in fact, struggles for power between major political elements at the highest level. The outstanding example of clumsy judicial interference prior to 1954 was the *Dred Scott* decision (1857) which declared the Missouri Compromise (1820) unconstitutional and thereby opened the whole of the western territories to the institution of slavery. The Court was then dominated by southerners and southern sympathizers, in contrast to the situation today in which the Warren Court, and indeed the whole of the federal judiciary, has been brought under the dominant influence of the dogmatic liberals. The *Dred Scott* decision, rather than settling the burning issue of the spread of slavery into the territories, as the Court thought would happen, brought the Court into great disrepute, intensified the bitterness between North and South, hastened the coming of the Civil War, and may well have made that war inevitable. "The power of the slaveholders," wrote one liberal historian, "had reached even into the Supreme Court of the United States—the one body that was popularly supposed to be above suspicion, influence or prejudice—and had dictated a legal opinion of sweeping importance."

The *Dred Scott* decision aroused the same strong emotions of anger and dismay among northern whites in 1857 that the *Brown* decree aroused in southern whites in 1954. Following the former decision, the prestige and influence of the Court in the North disappeared overnight, and the latter decision had the same effect on the white South. In 1857, Horace Greeley's widely read New York *Tribune* said that the *Dred Scott* decision "is entitled to just so much moral weight as would be the judgment of a majority of those congregated in any Washington barroom." And the New York *Independent,* a church-related paper, said: "If the people obey this decision, they disobey God." In the South of today, the United States Supreme Court and the lower federal courts have little or no moral authority or respect among the whites, and their decrees are enforced only by naked military power. While the Supreme Court apparently has had the support of the majority of the people of the North and West, in recent years the prestige of the Court has been ebbing, especially with the threat to introduce massive busing to achieve desegregation of public schools in states outside the South. Throughout the country the people are losing faith as the Court continues to sacrifice the interests of the responsible, law-abiding citizens, white and black, in favor of the liberal intellectuals and allied special interest groups on the left.

18

Can the Courts Be Contained?

> The judiciary . . . has no influence over the sword or the purse . . . and can take no active resolution whatever. It may truly be said to have neither FORCE nor WILL, but merely judgment; and must ultimately depend upon the aid of the executive arm even for the efficacy of its judgments.
> — Alexander Hamilton, *The Federalist,* No. 78 (1788)
>
> Of the three powers above mentioned, the judiciary is next to nothing.
> — Montesquieu, *Spirit of Laws* (1748)

ALEXANDER HAMILTON, even though a believer in a strong central government, would have been deeply shocked had he been able to foresee the present position of the federal judiciary and of the states in our constitutional system. America's version of Montesquieu's ideal commonwealth of limited powers, checks and balances, and the widest possible distribution of powers, has been turned upside down, with the ostensibly weakest of the three branches of the central government exercising overriding political power at the top. Many conservative Americans, after observing the activist course of the federal judiciary for more than three decades, still find unbelievable the prevailing state of constitutional anarchy. "It is strange, indeed," concluded the chief justices of thirty-six states meeting in conference in 1958, "to reflect that . . . one branch of one government—the Supreme Court—should attain the immense and, in many respects, dominant power which it now wields."

And what would Alexander Hamilton think today of his argument that the judiciary would have "neither FORCE nor WILL, but merely judgment" should he be here to observe the power available to the Supreme Court to enforce its decrees; and the judicial willfulness and lack of judgment of such Supreme Court justices as Earl Warren, Hugo L. Black and, above all, William O. Douglas? But Hamilton's concept of a harmless, quiescent judiciary was not absolute. Further on in his discussion he qualifies his views by stating that the judiciary must remain "truly distinct from both the legislature and the Executive." He concluded that "liberty can have nothing to fear from the judiciary alone, but would have everything to fear from its union with either [or both] of the other departments. . . ."

Hamilton here foresaw what has actually happened. Judicial activism has had the consistent support of the legislative branch since Roosevelt's second term and either the active support or the neutrality of the executive branch. A succession of weak Congresses and presidents, cowering under the lash of the intellectuals and other minority groups in the liberal-left coalition, has permitted the Supreme Court to seize the leadership in the legislative and law enforcement fields and has supported the Court in its invasion of many areas reserved to the states by the Constitution. The climax in this war against the states, carried on by a combination of the three branches of the federal government, came in 1965 when President Johnson with his cabinet appeared before a joint session of Congress to demand "civil rights" legislation in support of and supplementing Supreme Court decisions in this field, while five of the nine justices of the

Supreme Court, including the chief justice, sat in the front row applauding the president as he shouted the slogans of the "civil rights" mobs.

Since the *Brown* decision in 1954, many proposals have been made by conservatives in and out of Congress for containing the Supreme Court, either by constitutional amendment or by the use of existing authority, but the powers of the Court remain untouched and, in fact, continue to grow year by year. Congress has ample power to restrain the federal courts under the provisions of Article III of the Constitution, which is concerned with the judicial department. And in the amending process, described in Article V, Congress has the authority by two-thirds vote to propose amendments to the Constitution that would serve to curb the power of the courts, provided a proposed amendment were ratified by three-fourths of the states acting through the state legislatures or conventions. Within the last two decades, conservatives in Congress have attempted numerous times to restrain the Courts by legislation or constitutional amendment but have not been able to rally a sufficient number of votes.

Article V also provides for direct action on the part of the states to amend the Constitution. Upon the application of two-thirds of the state legislatures, Congress is required to call a convention for proposing amendments which must then be ratified by the legislatures of or by conventions in three-fourths of the states. Such a convention, which would have had the power of restraining the federal courts, was very nearly called in the 1960s, obtaining the approval of all but one of the necessary two-thirds of the state legislatures.

Article III of the Constitution states that: "The judicial power of the United States shall be vested in one Supreme Court, and in such inferior courts as the Congress may from time to time ordain and establish." But the Constitution specifically mentions only a single judicial officer, the chief justice. All of the associate justices are creatures of the executive and legislative branches, and their seats could be legally eliminated by the refusal of the president to nominate successors to fill vacancies, or the refusal of the Senate to approve presidential nominees, or by removal from office by impeachment. Furthermore, all of the lower federal courts exist by the will of Congress, for the Constitution left it to Congress to determine the extent of the lower court system. Here, too, Congress could constitutionally eliminate the whole of the federal lower court system by repeal of laws establishing the system, or by refusing to approve nominees to fill vacancies, or by impeachment and removal from office.

In the Constitutional Convention there were some who believed that all judicial power other than that lodged in the federal Supreme Court should rest in the state courts. This view was widely held in the states during the ratification controversy, forcing Hamilton to attempt to answer it in *Federalist* paper No. 81. Hamilton's principal objection was that "the prevalency of a local spirit may be found to disqualify the local tribunals for the jurisdiction of national causes . . ." Of course, national courts are equally disqualified for the jurisdiction of local causes. Perhaps Hamilton's opponents, the anti-Federalists, were right after all. Today, the lower federal courts never hesitate to invade the jurisdiction of the state courts, overturn state court decisions at will, and seem never to be willing to let a final decision be reached in a state court in those areas in which the federal courts have invaded state prerogatives.

While there is no likelihood that the federal lower court system will be abolished, it is probable that it will be sharply curtailed should a change in the political tide bring in a strongly conservative Congress. It appears that Parkinson's Law operates in the federal judiciary as it does in the federal administrative bureaucracy. In both agencies, "work expands to fill the time available for its completion." As our bloated federal lower court system has expanded into a vast network of district courts and courts of appeal, the judges have been kept busy finding work to do to justify their existence. They have gone far beyond their prescribed duties and let their real work languish while taking on the tasks of school administrators, social reformers, and protectors of criminals, pornographers and political agitators violating state laws. In March, 1970, the House of Representatives passed a bill to create fifty-four new federal district judgeships. Representative William M. Colmer of Mississippi, chairman of the House Rules Committee, opposed the bill because, he said, the additional judgeships would not be necessary had not the federal courts taken upon themselves the running of the schools. "So what we are going to have, in effect," Congressman Colmer stated, "if I may say so, are 54 more school administrators."

Perhaps the most readily available means of curbing the Supreme Court is provided for in Section 2 of Article III of the Constitution which delineates the Court's original jurisdiction and its appellate jurisdiction. Its original jurisdiction extends only to "cases affecting ambassadors, other public ministers, and consuls, and those in which a state shall be a party." Article III further states, "In all other cases the Supreme Court shall have appellate jurisdiction, both as to law and fact, with such exceptions and under such regulations as the Congress shall make." By terms of the Constitution, then, Congress could deny to the Court appellate jurisdiction in those areas in which the Court has abused its authority. Numerous reform measures have been introduced in Congress to accomplish just this—that is, for restricting federal court jurisdiction in certain areas such as legislative apportionment, criminal law, and school administration. None of these measures have become law because conservative sponsors have never been able to secure the necessary votes.

Numerous proposals for curbing the Court have been introduced in Congress in the form of constitutional amendments, but none have been approved. The most popular of the proposed amendments have been concerned with abolishing tenure-for-life of the justices and lower court judges and reducing tenure to more limited terms; and providing for the election of federal judges rather than their appointment.

David Lawrence and others have long championed repeal of the Fourteenth Amendment. This would be the most straightforward measure possible and would involve less meddling with the original consititutional structure. More than any type of action, it would cut the ground from under the Court's ambition to become a permanent center of political power. As we have seen, the Court's political power today is based almost wholly on the "due process" and "equal protection" clauses of the Fourteenth Amendment and the doctrine that this amendment makes the Bill of Rights binding upon the states. Furthermore, justice would be served by eliminating from our Constitution a tainted amendment approved by a rump Congress and never legally ratified.

With all of the possible lines of action for curbing the powers of the Supreme Court, reformers must come back to the reality that reform by statute or amendment is impossible as long as Congress is controlled by defenders of the Court's activism and as long as public opinion is swayed by the intellectuals in the communications media, academy, labor unions, and elsewhere. Every proposal for containing the Court has brought down upon the heads of conservative leaders in Congress verbal abuse from the law schools, the metropolitan newspapers and eminent labor leaders. The late Walter P. Reuther of the United Auto Workers, for example, in a speech to an NAACP audience, referred to Senator James O. Eastland of Mississippi in the following terms: "Eastland and his association of bigots don't understand the great social dynamic forces sweeping the world. We need to get through to the dark corners of their small mentalities on this." Bernard Schwartz, professor of law in New York University, dismissed criticisms of the Court as no more than "peculiar aberrations"; and the Washington *Post*, editorializing on an article of Governor James F. Byrnes of South Carolina critical of the Court, condemned Byrnes' "tired, tawdry arguments" and his "insensate bitterness" that would cause him "to stoop even to the absurd contention that the Court was subject in its [school segregation] decision to Communist influences." Apparently, the *Post* editor had not read Senator Eastland's Senate speech of May 26, 1955, revealing the Communist or Communist-front backgrounds of many of the authors of the social science treatises cited by Chief Justice Earl Warren in the *Brown* decree as "modern authority."

From a realistic political point of view, under present circumstances or in the foreseeable future, the only practical method of reforming the Supreme Court is to pack it, as President Richard M. Nixon is attempting to do as this is written. Whatever criticisms may be made of Mr. Nixon's conservatism in some areas, there can be no doubt that he is honestly determined to turn the Court around by filling vacancies with the the most conservative men he can find who are likely to win the approval of the Senate. Mr. Nixon has recognized that his power to appoint Supreme Court justices is one of his most important, because in fulfilling this duty his influence will be felt long after his own term as president has ended.

In attempting to pack the Court, President Nixon is following a historic and time-honored precedent. In the Washington and Adams administrations, at the very beginning of our national life under the Constitution, the Supreme Court and lower federal courts were packed with Federalist judges, including John Marshall who was appointed chief justice in the last month of the Adams administration. Marshall remained on the Court for a third of a century, exerting a strong centralizing influence on national affairs long after the Federalist party had ceased to exist and political power had passed to the party of his bitter enemies, Thomas Jefferson and Andrew Jackson. Jackson and his Democratic successors were able to pack the Court with men of their own party who dominated the Court until the Civil War period;

and Lincoln and Grant packed the Court with Republicans during the war and the Reconstruction era that followed. Franklin D. Roosevelt attempted to pack the Court in a most direct manner by proposing to raise the number of justices from nine to fifteen, but he was unable to secure the support of the majority of the Senate. He packed the Court, nevertheless, because in his second term he was able to fill seven vacancies within a period of four years with men of his own views.

Court-packing has its hazards, as some presidents have discovered. President Dwight D. Eisenhower appointed Earl Warren to the chief justiceship, thinking that the then governor of California was at least a "moderate," which in modern journalese means one who is somewhere to the right of William O. Douglas and to the left of Senator Barry Goldwater. However, when Chief Justice Warren assumed office he moved down to the extreme left end of the bench and took a seat alongside Douglas and Hugo L. Black to form the radical wing of the Court, much to the dismay of the president and the conservatives of the country. Earl Warren was a disaster to the political health and the domestic tranquility of the nation.

President Richard M. Nixon must have had a moment of doubt when his first appointee, Chief Justice Warren E. Burger, cast his first vote by joining his colleagues in a unanimous ruling in the Mississippi schools case. In this decision, the Supreme Court reversed the Fifth Circuit Court of Appeals which had given certain Mississippi school districts a few months grace to allow them time to develop plans for carrying out the Court's latest integration order. This delay of several months had been requested of the Fifth Circuit Court by the Nixon administration, and when the NAACP appealed the circuit court order to the Supreme Court, the Department of Justice, for the first time in many years, found itself on the opposite side of the table from the NAACP counsel.

Can the Courts Be Contained?

The Supreme Court, with Burger presiding, was now in one of its angry, petulant moods induced by the continued opposition to its school decrees. Its unanimous decision denying the request for delay gave the Nixon administration a peremptory lesson in judicial supremacy; chided the court of appeals for granting the delay; and ordered the Mississippi school districts, as well as other public school systems in the South, "to terminate dual school systems at once and to operate now and hereafter only unitary schools." The Court had scanned the heavens for signs, gazed into its crystal ball, consulted the sibylline book, and after throwing a pinch of salt over its left shoulder, had found that the Supreme Court order of 1955, to desegregate "with all deliberate speed," was not in the Constitution after all. This doctrine, the Court found, "is no longer constitutionally permissible," and all public school systems must begin "immediately [day after tomorrow?] to operate as unitary school systems," a term which the Court did not bother to define with any precision.

After Burger's participation in this unanimous decision, some commentators expressed the opinion that he had begun his Court service by giving the Nixon administration a slap in the face. Possibly what Burger had done was to let the members of the club, his colleagues on the bench, know that he did not intend to add to the Court's embarrassment in being unable to force the American public to accept the Court's school segregation/desegregation decrees as the law of the land. One of the more fanatical defenders of the Warren Court and critics of the Burger appointment, Professor Fred Rodell of the Yale Law School, suggested that Chief Justice Burger would probably have dissented in the Mississippi schools case had he been able to persuade at least one other justice to dissent with him. Professor Rodell was here accusing the chief justice of being too cowardly to vote his own convictions and being fearful that he would look "damn silly," to employ Rodell's words, if he dissented alone. This can be dismissed, however, as the prejudice of Burger's most extreme and virulent critic, possessed of the instincts of his judicial heroes, Earl Warren, Hugo L. Black, and William O. Douglas.

After the resignation of Associate Justice Abe Fortas, President Nixon nominated and the Senate rejected two federal court judges from the South, Clement F. Haynsworth of South Carolina and G. Harrold Carswell of Florida. Nixon next nominated in April, 1970, Judge Harry A. Blackmun of Minnesota, then sitting on the Eighth Circuit Court of Appeals. He was found less obnoxious by the "civil rights" forces in the Senate and was approved. In 1971, with the retirement of Hugo L. Black and John M. Harlan, Nixon nominated and the Senate confirmed two men generally considered to be conservatives. These were Lewis F. Powell, Jr., of Richmond, Virginia, former president of the American Bar Association, and William H. Rehnquist of Arizona, assistant attorney general.

After Burger and Blackmun joined the Court, they voted consistently with the other members in handing down unanimous decisions upholding the lower courts in all school desegregation decrees. Burger even wrote the opinion in the Charlotte-Mecklenburg County case and related cases upholding lower court decrees ordering massive busing across adjoining city and county school district boundaries in order to achieve maximum mixing of the races in the public schools in city and suburbs. It is difficult to understand how judges who see such a requirement in the Constitution can be described as conservatives, especially when the evidence is overwhelming that the Supreme Court's race-mixing decrees are causing anarchy in the schools, heightened racial tensions, a revolt of the taxpayers, and a general breakdown in the educational process.

Perhaps the actions of Burger and Blackmun—and the other two Nixon appointees may well join them—prove the truth of the Chinese proverb: "He who rides the tiger can never dismount." Neither the Nixon appointees nor other members of the Court who might be inclined to change their minds will ever be able to dismount from the liberal school desegregation tiger except at the risk of being torn to pieces by the intellectuals and allied "civil rights" forces. Any attempt to dismount would result in an awful slaughter led by the screaming NAACP, the New York *Times* and Washington *Post*, the American Civil Liberties Union, Americans for Democratic Action, National Council of Churches, the law school faculties, and very nearly the whole of the academy. And these would be the more moderate of the forces crying havoc and demanding the blood of the transgressors.

If the justices continue their refusal to dismount, then they will eventually be pulled off the back of the tiger by the force of public opinion. The news reports today indicate clearly that public patience with the meddling of the federal courts in public school administration is running out. Political tides can turn rapidly, and what is tolerated or even applauded today may be treated with contempt tomorrow. The justices of the Supreme Court as well as those of the lower federal courts might profit from a study of the prohibition movement and the revived Ku Klux Klan in the earlier decades of this century. The political power of the prohibition and Klan forces had grown so great that they virtually dominated the Democratic convention of 1924, or at least were able to obstruct and confound it for many days; but less than a decade later any political leader who advocated either the prohibition or Klan programs would have been laughed out of public life.

No doubt the great error of the prohibition and Klan movements of yesterday and the judicial activism of the Warren Court of more recent times is that each attempted to apply rationalist solutions to problems in human conduct which are basically religious problems. While the Klan is best known and condemned today for its bias against certain groups, its stated purpose was to raise the level of public and private morality by gaining control of and manipulating the machinery of government. As we know, the prohibitionists attempted to solve the ages-old liquor problem by the application of the police power of the national state. And today the federal courts are attempting to solve a centuries-old problem in race relations by judicial fiat based on a reckless reading of the Constitution. The political adventurism of the prohibition and Klan movements dashed itself to pieces upon the hard rock of American common sense. There is much reason to believe that judicial activism of the past several decades is on the verge of destroying itself in the same manner.

Index

A

Abington Township v. Schempp (see *Schempp-Murray* cases)
Acheson, Dean, 40, 46-7, 53
Adamson v. California, 54, 68
Allen, James E., Jr., 138-42
Alsop, Joseph, 30, 92
American Anthropological Association, 35
American Bar Association, 101, 102, 121
American Civil Liberties Union (ACLU), 59, 75, 126, 149-50, 165
American Historical Association, 13
American Jewish Congress, 38, 59
Americans for Democratic Action (ADA), 75, 150, 165
An American Dilemma, 31-4, 92
Anti-Defamation League, 150
Anti-Saloon League, 45
Asch, Sidney H., *Civil Rights & Responsibilities Under the Constitution*, 43-4

B

Babbitt, Irving, *Rousseau and Romanticism*, 90-1, 94
Bacon, Francis, 91
Baker, Bobby, 133-4
Baker v. Carr, 64
Baldwin v. Missouri, 59
Barron v. Baltimore, 52, 67, 68
Bayh, Birch, 142
Bill of Rights, 40-1, 44-5, 52, 66-74, 116, 160
Bill of Rights, Its Origin and Meaning, The, 40-2, 44, 46
Bingham, John A., 18, 54, 68

Black, Hugo L., 6, 33, 41, 54, 65, 68, 71, 77, 79-80, 98, 122-5, 130, 156, 162, 164
Blackmun, Harry A., 164
Boas, Frank, 34-6, 39
Bolling v. Sharpe, 13
Bozell, L. Brent, *The Warren Revolution*, 7, 23, 77
Brameld, Theodore, 32
Brant, Irving, *The Bill of Rights, Its Origin and Meaning*, 40-2, 44, 46
Brown v. Board of Education of Topeka, 7-8, 12-18, 22-9, 31-9, 44, 53, 56, 61-4, 88, 91-3, 105-6, 116, 121, 123, 130, 140, 151, 153, 157, 161
Browning, Orville, 49-50
Burger, Warren E., 135, 146-7, 162-4
Burke, Edmund, 21, 30, 94, 11, 117-9
Burnham, James, 76
Burton, Harold H., 28, 29
Busing, 61, 63, 64, 141, 146, 164
Byrd, Harry F., Sr., 42
Byrnes, James F., 122, 160-1

C

Calhoun, John C., 42
California Communist cases, 80-1
Cantwell v. Connecticut, 72-3
Cardozo, Benjamin N., 70
Carmichael, Peter A., *The South and Segregation*, 28, 36-7, 66, 68
Carnegie Foundation, 33
Carswell, G. Harrold, 164
Center for the Study of Democratic Institutions, 128-9
Chain, Isidor, 38

167

Characteristics of the American Negro, 37
Charlotte-Mecklenburg County Case, 164
Christianity, 85-9, 94, 96-7
Civil Rights Act of 1866, 14-17, 23, 52, 53
Civil Rights Act of 1875, 55
Civil Rights Cases, 55
Civil Rights & Responsibilities Under the Constitution, 43
Clark, Kenneth B., 32-3, 36
Clark, Ramsey, 98
Clark, Tom C., 28-9, 74, 79, 81
Clay, Henry, 42
Clifford, Clark, 134
Coffin, William Sloane, 149-50
Colmer, William M., 159
Columbia Broadcasting System (CBS), 142
Commentaries, 72
Commentary, 84
Communists, 4, 5, 32-4, 58, 68, 75-81, 85, 87, 95, 99, 109, 123
Congress of Industrial Organizations (CIO), 128
Congressional Government, 79
Cooper v. Aaron, 24
Criminal law cases, 65
Cruikshank Decision (see *United States v. Cruikshank*)
Cumming v. Richmond County Board of Education, 61

D

Daily Worker, 32
Davidson, Donald, 57
Davis, Angela, 98
Davis, Jefferson, 54
Davis, John W., 28
Descartes, Rene, 91
Deutscher, Max, 38
Dewey, John, 25
Dictionary of American Biography, 53-4

Douglas, William O., 6, 31, 33, 71, 77, 108, 122-3, 127-30, 132, 156, 162, 164
Dred Scott v. Sandford, 3, 153-4
Drury, Allen, 133
Du Bois, W.E.B., 34

E

Eastland, James O., 32-5, 160-1
Eisenhower, Dwight, 4, 6, 9, 105, 117, 162
Engel v. Vitale, 73-4
Ethridge, Tom, 147

F

Fascism, 85
Fauntroy, Walter, 143
Federalist, The, 75, 155-6, 158
Fifteenth Amendment, 15
Fifth Amendment, 13, 28, 29, 65
Finch, Robert H., 141
First Amendment, 43, 66-74
Forbes, 102
Fortas, Abe, 5, 42, 129, 132-7, 147, 164
Fourteenth Amendment, 11-18, 23, 26, 28, 29, 41, 47, 49-74, 115-6, 160
Frankfurter, Felix, 28, 29, 31, 33, 64, 77, 79, 104, 122-7, 130
Frazier, E. Franklin, 32, 34
Freedman, Max, 126
French Revolution, 60, 86, 95-6, 119,

G

Gaines case (see *Missouri ex rel. Gaines v. Canada*)
Gitlow v. New York, 66, 68-9
Gnosticism, 85-9
Goldberg, Arthur, 134
Goldwater, Barry, 162

INDEX

Gong Lum v. Rice, 61, 62
Graham, Katherine, 103
Graham, Philip L., 103
Green v. New Kent County, Va., 63, 140
Greenberg, Jack, 151

H

Hamilton, Alexander, 155-6, 158
Harlan, John M., 164
Harper's, 79
Hart, Jeffrey, 41
Harvard Educational Review, 35
Haynsworth, Clement F., 164
Hobbes, Thomas, 3, 16, 91
Holmes, Oliver Wendell, 59, 107
House Un-American Activities Committee, 36, 78, 99, 123
Howard, Jacob, 17, 18, 53, 54
Howe, Harold, II, 139-41
Howlett, Duncan, 108, 125
Hughes, Charles Evans, 80
Hyman, Sidney, 88

I

Intellectuals, 6, 8, 20, 36, 41-7, 57-60, 69, 70, 82-9, 90-100, 156, 160, 165

J

Jackson, Andrew, 42, 117, 161
Jackson, James E., Jr., 34
Jackson, Robert H., 122-3, 130-1
Jackson (Miss.) *Clarion-Ledger,* 147, 152
Jefferson, Thomas, 8, 25, 42, 109, 117, 132, 146
Jensen, Arthur R., 35
Johnson, Andrew, 51
Johnson, Charles S., 34
Johnson, Frank M., Jr., 147-9

Johnson, Lyndon B., 10, 14, 98, 117, 124, 132-5, 139, 156
Journal of Psychology, 37-8

K

Katz v. United States, 65
Kelly, Alfred H., 13-19, 23, 53
Kennedy, Edward M., 125, 142
Kennedy, John F., 10, 88-9, 104, 106, 117, 139
Kennedy, Robert F., 115
Keppel, Francis, 139-41
Kilpatrick, James J., 24, 139
King, Martin Luther, Jr., 38, 39
Kirk, Russell, 52
Klineberg, Otto, *Characteristics of the American Negro,* 37
Kotinsky, Ruth, 37
Ku Klux Klan, 123, 130, 152, 165-6

L

Lawrence, David, 15, 132, 160
League of Women Voters, 150
Life, 136
Lincoln, Abraham, 54, 117, 145, 162
Lippmann, Walter, 78
Lord, John Wesley, 115

M

McCarthy, Eugene, 142
McCarthy, Joseph R., 76, 104, 105
McGovern, George, 142
Madison, James, 75
Marbury v. Madison, 24-5
Marcuse, Herbert, 97-8
Marshall, John, 3, 24, 25, 67, 121, 161
Marshall, Thurgood, 14-18, 141, 151

Marx, Karl, 85, 86, 88, 95
Meyer, Agnes, 21, 22, 101-11
Meyer, Eugene, 101-4, 110-11
Miller, Samuel F., 55
Minton, Sherman, 28, 29
Mississippi Schools case, 152, 162-3
Missouri ex rel. Gaines v. Canada, 60-2
Modern Age, 82
Montesquieu, 155
Murphy, Frank, 122
Murray v. Curlett (see *Schempp-Murray* cases)
Myrdal, Gunnar, *An American Dilemma*, 31-4, 92

N

National Association for the Advancement of Colored People (NAACP), 12-19, 22, 23, 26, 33, 34, 53, 59, 88, 126, 128, 139, 151, 162, 165
National Council of Churches (NCC), 96-7, 150-1, 165
National Education Association (NEA), 138-9, 150
National Review, 46, 76, 86
Naziism, 85
Near v. Minnesota, 69
Nelson case (see *Pennsylvania v. Nelson*)
Neuburger, Richard, 98
New Republic, 79
Newsweek, 103
New York *Independent*, 153
New York *Times*, 40, 42, 43, 46, 47, 85, 99, 165
New York *Tribune*, 153
Niemeyer, Gerhardt, 86
Ninth Amendment, 44, 70
Nixon, Richard M., 4, 135, 138-9, 141, 161-5

P

Palko v. Connecticut, 67, 70
Parvin Foundation, 128-9
Pearson, Drew, 109-10, 133
Pennsylvania v. Nelson, 76-8
Personality in the Making, 36-7
Philpott, Harry, 149
Plato, 88
Plessy v. Ferguson, 56, 61
Porter, Paul, 135-6
Powell, Lewis F., 164
Prohibition, 93, 165-6

R

Radical Republicans, 15-17, 49-54, 67
Rationalism, 90-4
Reconstruction, 1865-1877, The Era of, 53
Reed, Stanley, 122-3, 130
Reflections on the Revolution in France, 21, 94, 119
Rehnquist, William H., 164
Reuther, Walter P., 160
Reynolds, Don, 133-4
Roberts, Owen J., 72-3
Robespierre, Maximilien de, 60, 96, 115
Rodell, Fred, 163-4
Romanticism, 85, 90-1, 94-6
Roosevelt, Eleanor, 89, 106, 108
Roosevelt, Franklin D., 58, 60, 83, 121-31, 156, 162
Rousseau, Jean Jacques, 85-6, 90-1, 94-6, 115
Rousseau and Romanticism, 90
Rowan, Carl, 143
Russell, Richard B., 42
Rutledge, Wiley B., 122

S

Sanford, Edward T., 68-9

INDEX   171

Santayana, George, 18-19
Schempp-Murray cases, 21, 73-4
Schlesinger, Arthur M., 88, 115
Schwartz, Bernard, 160
Science, politics and gnosticism, 86-9
Second Reconstruction, 50, 60
Slaughterhouse Cases, 54
Smith, Howard W., 77
Smith Act, 77, 80-1
Social sciences, 18, 27-9, 30-9, 45-6, 92
Socialism, 85, 96
Socrates, 82, 103
Sophists, 82, 83
South and Segregation, The, 28, 36-7, 66, 68
Southern Conference for Human Welfare, 123
Stampp, Kenneth M., *The Era of Reconstruction, 1865-1877*, 53
Stanlis, Peter, 82
Stevens, Thaddeus, 15
Stevenson, Adlai, 105, 106, 108
Story, Joseph, *Commentaries*, 72
Sweatt v. Painter, 62
Swisher, Carl Brent, 146
Sulzberger, Arthur Ochs, 43

T

Taft, Robert A., 42
Tenth Amendment, 24, 44, 61, 70, 88, 115
Time, 103
Tonsor, Stephen J., 45-6
Trumball, Lyman, 16

U

United States v. Cruikshank, 68
U.S. News and World Report, 15
University of California, 98-9
Urban, Irene, 47

V

Vinson, Fred M., 7, 28-9
Virginia Law Review, 146
Voegelin, Eric, *Science, Politics and Gnosticism*, 86-9

W

Wall Street Journal, 114
Washington Post, 21, 42, 46, 85, 99, 101-4, 106-7, 110-11, 115, 125, 142-3, 160-1, 165
Watkins v. United States, 5, 78-80
Webster, Daniel, 42, 148-9
Wallace, Mike, 142
Warren, Earl, 3-11, 21-9, 33, 37, 41, 78, 80, 89, 91-3, 101-20, 125-7, 134-5, 146-7, 156, 161-2, 164
Warren Revolution, The, 7, 23,77
Washington, George, 12
Washington, Walter, 143
Washington Afro-American, 123
Wesberry v. Sanders, 64
Wilkerson, Doxie, 34
Wilson, James F., 16
Wilson, Woodrow, *Congressional Government*, 79
Wirtz, W. Willard, 108
Witmer, Helen L., 37
Wolfson, Louis, 136